Starting a Movement

BUILDING CULTURE FROM THE INSIDE OUT IN PROFESSIONAL LEARNING COMMUNITIES

KENNETH C. WILLIAMS
TOM HIERCK

Solution Tree | Press

a division of

Solution Tree

555 North Morton Street
Bloomington, IN 47404
800.733.6786 (toll free) / 812.336.7700
FAX: 812.336.7790

email: info@solution-tree.com
solution-tree.com

Visit **go.solution-tree.com/plcbooks** to download the reproducibles in this book.

Printed in the United States of America

19   18   17   9   10

FSC
www.fsc.org
MIX
Paper from
responsible sources
FSC® C011935

Library of Congress Cataloging-in-Publication Data

Williams, Kenneth C.

  Starting a movement : building culture from the inside out in professional learning communities / by Kenneth C. Williams and Tom Hierck.

       pages cm

  Includes bibliographical references and index.

  ISBN 978-1-936764-66-2 (perfect bound) 1. Professional learning communities. 2. Teaching teams. 3. Teachers--Professional relationships. 4. Teachers--In-service training. 5. Educational leadership. I. Title.

  LB1731.W46 2015

  371.14'8--dc23

                              2015014974

Solution Tree
Jeffrey C. Jones, CEO
Edmund M. Ackerman, President

Solution Tree Press
President: Douglas M. Rife
Editorial Director: Lesley Bolton
Managing Production Editor: Caroline Weiss
Senior Production Editor: Suzanne Kraszewski
Copy Editor: Miranda Addonizio
Proofreader: Elisabeth Abrams
Cover Designer: Rian Anderson
Text Designer: Abigail Bowen

This book is dedicated to my wife, Nicole, and my two kids, Adam and Mia, who love me, encourage me, put up with me, keep me grounded, and honor my wiring. They are the single greatest reason I'm grateful when I awaken. They are my why.

I also dedicate this book to my parents, Carl and Suzanne Williams, and sisters, Keisha White and Carllie Jaxen, whose unconditional love and encouragement still make me feel like a wide-eyed five-year-old who just learned that he can do anything he puts his mind to. To teachers I've encountered in several stages of my life: I thank you for literally speaking vision into my life and challenging me to achieve things I didn't think possible.

To my second-grade teacher, Sister Mary Claire, who was the first teacher to make me feel like a million bucks; my seventh-grade teacher, Eleanor Fryer, who told me at age eleven I'd attend Morehouse College and explained why; to Gloria Wade Gayles, who decided I needed to be a teacher (after I spent $300 on law school applications); and, finally, to Rick DuFour. To paraphrase a quote by Howard Thurman, Rick holds above my head a crown that he challenges me to grow tall enough to wear. This book exists because of his unyielding faith in me and his vision for me.

—Kenneth C. Williams

Being a leader means being a learner. I am indebted to many people for providing me with the opportunity to lead and, more importantly, for providing feedback as I was leading that helped and encouraged my growth. From students I taught and coached, to the woman with whom I share my life, leaders and peers who I worked alongside, my three children, and the hundreds of educators I now meet with regularly; thanks for the insights you shared, the reminders you provided, and the support that has always been evident.

And, of course, to my four grandchildren, Isabella, Leah, Liam, and Kaiden: as you grow and learn, I find myself doing the same. Thanks for being such great teachers!

—Tom Hierck

Acknowledgments

This book would not be possible without the support of a collaborative team of passionate and purpose-driven people. We would like to thank the entire Solution Tree family, led by our colleague, mentor, and friend, Jeff Jones. We owe a debt of gratitude to Douglas Rife, our editor, Sue Kraszewski, and the publishing team of Solution Tree. They have been patient, supportive, and encouraging.

We thank so many colleagues and friends we've gained through our virtual professional learning networks. We thank fellow Solution Tree associates. We appreciate the efforts of school leaders and teacher leaders working in schools to build a culture of collective responsibility. We thank practitioners Jenny McGown, Paula Maeker, Cory Radisch, Lisa Blackstock, Greg Wolcott, Bethany Schill, and Rosa Isiah for allowing us residence in their minds and schools. They are models for clarity of shared purpose, transparency, collaboration, and "coachability." A special nod to our dear friend Nicole Vagle. We are eternally grateful for her bringing this collaboration together.

Our work is largely influenced by the trailblazing efforts of Anthony Muhammad and Mike Mattos. We are blessed to count them as colleagues and honored to have them as friends and mentors.

Our work is possible due to the enduring work of Rick DuFour, Becky DuFour, and Bob Eaker. They have made professional learning communities (PLCs) household practice in schools across North

America. From the very beginning, the movement they started has been about helping schools, in the midst of a thousand distractions, to ensure high levels of learning for all students. Our purpose is to support their great work. Rick, Becky, and Bob are the roots of the PLC family tree. Their impact on our work is profound, their giving is boundless, and we are honored to count them as mentors, colleagues, friends, and family.

Solution Tree Press would like to thank the following reviewers:

Jason Andrews
Superintendent
Windsor Central School
    District
Windsor, New York

Tom Bailey
Principal
Hailey Elementary School
Hailey, Idaho

Adele Bovard
Superintendent
Webster Central School
    District
Webster, New York

Joe Cuddemi
Principal
Kinard Core Knowledge
    Middle School
Fort Collins, Colorado

Dr. Bruce Hibbard
Superintendent
New Albany Floyd County
    Schools
New Albany, Indiana

Keith Mispagel
Superintendent of Schools
USD 207
Fort Leavenworth, Kansas

Cheryl O'Leary
Principal
Garden Hills Elementary
Champaign, Illinois

Dr. Randall W. Peterson
Principal
Eastview High School
Apple Valley, Minnesota

Denny Roehm
Principal
West Middle School
Portage, Michigan

Scott Schiller
Principal
Southside Elementary School
Powell, Wyoming

Marilyn Sylvester
Principal
Longleaf Elementary School
Melbourne, Florida

Table of Contents

Visit **go.solution-tree.com/PLCbooks** to download the reproducibles in this book.

Chapter 2
What Is Authentic Alignment?

Chapter 3

Exploring: The Why

Chapter 7
Communication: Stories and Celebrations

Epilogue
Moving From Posters to Practice

References and Resources

Index

About the Authors

Kenneth C. Williams began his career in education in 1992 and has been a classroom teacher, assistant principal, and school principal in both Maryland and Georgia. Kenneth successfully led two schools through the professional learning communities transformation. He began speaking, training, and consulting full time in 2008 and has worked with schools at all levels across North America. Known for combining equal parts heart, humor, and hammer, Ken delivers proven, practical solutions in a very relatable style. He is passionate about strengthening the cultural core of schools so improved learning for students and staff can emerge. His work with schools is about moving from "pockets of excellence" to building a culture of learning for all. He's helped hundreds of schools see past their current circumstances and chart a course to become the embodiment of their ideal school.

His leadership was crucial to creating a successful professional learning community at Damascus Elementary School in Maryland, a challenged school that needed a new direction. The results of his efforts can be seen across all grade levels. Over a two-year period, the school's state standardized test scores revealed a significant increase in the percentage of students performing at proficient and advanced levels. The process of building a PLC at E. J. Swint in Jonesboro, Georgia, continues thanks to Kenneth's work in laying a solid foundation in this underserved community.

He is the author of *Creating Physical & Emotional Security in Schools* (2nd edition), and is a contributor to *The Collaborative Administrator*.

Kenneth earned a bachelor of arts from Morehouse College, a master of science from the University of Bridgeport, and an administration and supervision certificate from Bowie State University.

To learn more about Kenneth's work, visit www.unfoldthesoul .com. You may also follow him on Twitter @unfoldthesoul and on Facebook at Unfold the Soul.

Tom Hierck has been an experienced educator since 1983, serving as assistant superintendent of School District Number 46 (Sunshine Coast) in Gibsons, British Columbia, and principal in the Kootenay Lake School District in British Columbia. He also served with the Ministry of Education. Tom is a compelling presenter, infusing his message of hope with strategies culled from the real world. He has presented to schools and districts across North America with a message of celebration for educators seeking to make a difference in the lives of students. Tom's dynamic presentations explore the importance of positive learning environments and the role of assessment to improve student learning. His belief that "every student is a success story waiting to be told" has led him to work with teachers and administrators to create positive school cultures and build effective relationships that facilitate learning for all students. Tom was a recipient of the Queen's Golden Jubilee Medallion, presented by the premier and lieutenant-governor of British Columbia, for being a recognized leader in the field of public education. Tom earned his master's degree at Gonzaga University and his bachelor's degree and teacher certification at the University of British Columbia.

This book is Tom's sixth publication for Solution Tree. He started his writing career with chapters in *The Teacher as Assessment Leader* and *The Principal as Assessment Leader*. The best-selling *Pyramid of Behavior Interventions: Seven Keys to a Positive Learning Environment* was followed by *Uniting Academic and Behavior Interventions: Solving the Skill or Will Dilemma* and *Strategies for Mathematics Instruction and Intervention, 6–8*.

To learn more about Tom's work, visit www.tomhierck.com, follow @thierck on Twitter, or visit Tom Hierck on Facebook and LinkedIn.

To book Kenneth or Tom for professional development, contact pd@solution-tree.com.

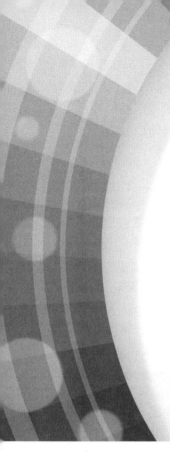

Introduction

Ready, Set, Stall . . .

> There is a difference between interest and commitment. When you're interested in doing something, you do it only when it is convenient. When you're committed to something, you accept no excuses, only results.
>
> —KENNETH BLANCHARD

As the Professional Learning Communities at Work™ (PLC) initiative gained momentum in the early 2000s, many educators wondered:

- If PLCs were a fad
- If we could really expect all students to learn at high levels
- If working interdependently through collaboration was really best practice

Heated debates arose on whether collaboration really was possible and a desirable way to achieve the stated goals of a school. Detractors vehemently defended the practice of teaching in isolation—not because of any research that supports it, but because it is easier than collaboration. It's true: working together is a lot more challenging than working alone. Focusing on what we as teachers *can do* instead of on what we *don't have* requires a collective commitment.

1

Since the early years of PLCs, many success stories have helped change the perception of the process from a model that challenges the status quo to a highly regarded framework in which:

- We accept teacher collaboration as best practice to improve student learning and instructional practice
- Educators embrace the notion that teaching hasn't occurred until learning has

Becoming a PLC still presents some challenges to the status quo and an ongoing need for paradigm shifts, but educators by and large agree that the structure offers our best hope for significant school improvement.

Early in the PLC movement, Bruce Joyce and Beverly Showers (1995) noted that "the development of a learning community of educators is itself a major cultural change that will spawn many others" (p. 3). Likewise, Linda Darling-Hammond (1996) recommends that "schools be restructured to become genuine learning organizations for both students and teachers: organizations that respect learning, honor teaching, and teach for understanding" (p. 198).

Melanie S. Morrissey (2000) notes the benefits:

> [PLCs] offer an infrastructure to create the supportive cultures and conditions necessary for achieving significant gains in teaching and learning. Professional learning communities provide opportunities for professional staff to look deeply into the teaching and learning process and to learn how to become more effective in their work with students.

As PLCs gained popularity, more researchers began to pay attention. Another study asserts:

> [PLCs] hold considerable promise for supporting implementation of improvement initiatives and the progress of educational reform more generally. An effective professional learning community has the

capacity to promote and sustain the learning of all professionals in the school community with the collective purpose of enhancing pupil learning. (Stoll et al., 2006, pp. 3–4)

As Michael Barber and Mona Mourshed (2009) note, "PLCs are an indication of a broader trend toward professional development that is increasingly collaborative, data-driven, and peer facilitated, all with a focus on classroom practice" (p. 30). Other findings suggest that "participation in a professional community with one's colleagues is an integral part of professional learning that impacts positively on students" (Timperley, 2008, p. 19).

In addition, many organizations have endorsed the PLC movement. The National Board for Professional Teaching Standards (n.d.) has developed professional standards for accomplished teaching. The organization's fifth proposition is that "teachers are members of learning communities" who collaborate with others to improve student learning.

The National Council of Teachers of Mathematics (NCTM; 2008) has called on math leaders to:

1. Ensure teachers work interdependently as a professional learning community to guarantee continuous improvement and gains in student achievement

2. Create the support and structures necessary to implement a professional learning community

3. Ensure a systemic implementation of a professional learning community throughout all aspects of the mathematics curriculum, instruction, and assessment at the school, district, or regional level

Likewise, the National Council of Teachers of English (NCTE) passed a resolution supporting PLCs. Its 2006 position paper argues that PLCs make teaching more rewarding and combat the problem of educators leaving the profession. It notes:

Effective professional development fosters collegial relationships, creating professional communities where teachers share knowledge and treat each other with respect. Within such communities, teacher inquiry and reflection can flourish, and research shows that teachers who engage in collaborative professional development feel confident and well prepared to meet the demands of teaching. (NCTE, 2006, p. 10)

While PLCs receive much external support, the challenge for schools is internal. Regardless of the locale, demographics, or pressures facing a school or district, the title of this chapter identifies one common threat to the success of PLC implementation: ready, set, stall. Schools and districts may set out to implement the PLC model with great energy and a lot of hope. However, if the work feels like one more thing to do then it is just that; a shift from *doing* a PLC (compliance) to *becoming* a PLC (commitment) is necessary.

If schools and districts don't evolve from compliance to commitment, then they won't see the results of their work: improved learning for both students and adults. We contend that belief follows behavior. Though it's human nature to need to see success before believing, success comes about by first examining, exploring, envisioning, and committing to agreed-on, high-leverage best practices. Early in any process, one expects to see more compliance than commitment. The problem emerges when schools remain trapped in a cycle of compliance without evolving toward commitment. Unless something changes, these schools never transform into true PLCs.

Even in schools with the best of intentions, those that find the PLC process stalling have almost always failed to build a culture of *collective responsibility*—the shared belief that the primary responsibility of each member of the organization is to ensure high levels of learning for every student (Buffum, Mattos, & Weber, 2012; DuFour, DuFour, & Eaker, 2008).

The Foundation of Your PLC

This book focuses on exploring the culture of your school and the importance of connecting with the *why* of your work. The why has nothing to do with deadlines, checklists, and data, and everything to do with how engagement in your work is aligned to your fundamental purpose: high levels of learning for all. For the PLC model to catch on within a school culture, the implementation must be deep and authentic. Catching on is what moves a school from doing a PLC to becoming a PLC. As Robert Eaker and Janel Keating (2008) observe, "While the term 'professional learning community' has traveled easily, actually transforming a school to function as a professional learning community requires much more than a superficial understanding of the concept and feeble attempts at reorganizing" (p. 15).

So how do you tackle the challenge of transitioning from a culture of compliance to a culture of commitment—from doing a PLC to becoming a PLC? The first step is to understand your current reality to figure out why your school improvement efforts are stalling. When you take responsibility for the state of your culture, it gives you an opportunity to learn from it, and you are then empowered to build a new culture.

Avoiding Mission Drift

In the world of nonprofits, a common term to describe an organization's movement away from its mission is *mission drift*. This is a pervasive issue for schools seeking to become PLCs as well. What we find fascinating is that this drift isn't due to the lack of a mission statement; in fact, all the schools we've worked with have had a mission statement or some form of guiding statements or principles. It might be that few can remember the mission statement, but most educators proudly proclaim its existence. Staff members simply drift away from a clear understanding of it as their day-to-day work moves away from the core focus of the school. What causes this drift to become so pervasive it's expected? What keeps the mission from becoming part of the fabric of a school's culture?

Drift happens when schools don't live their mission—often when educators unconsciously separate the mission from the work. It's not about a lack of commitment or investment; it is about a lack of commitment to or investment in the right things. We seek to shape a new paradigm, to help schools redirect their focus to what matters most, which isn't increasing test scores. What matters most is creating a school with an unrelenting focus on learning for all. To do that we must consider the current state of education and its complete focus on accountability, scores, and testing—to the detriment of everything else.

In our work in schools, we often hear teachers say they have given up the good stuff (engaging instruction, interesting activities—the fun of learning) to teach to the test. When teacher evaluations are partially based on student test results from an external exam, it's easy to see how the focus can shift in that direction. Teachers must reconnect with the reasons they became educators—reasons that doubtless had little to do with achieving the highest results on an external assessment. Think about what drove you to become an educator as you engage in the following activity.

Why Did You Become an Educator?

The following questions are adapted from the work of Yvette Jackson (2011) in *The Pedagogy of Confidence*. Take a few minutes, alone or with your team, to honestly consider each of the following questions about why you became an educator.

1. What made you feel you had something to offer students to help them learn?

2. Remember your first year of teaching and the hope and desire you had to reach students. What did that motivate you to do?

3. What was your first concrete evidence of success in your teaching, and how did it influence your passion and embolden you to use your gifts to unlock the gifts in your students? What were those aptitudes or talents you acted on?

4. Think back to the students on whom you had the most profound impact. How did you engage them?

5. What did it feel like when you realized you had, in fact, made an impact?

We have asked these questions of many different groups of educators from many states and provinces, from schools with differing demographics, and across the socioeconomic spectrum. In our experience, few to no educators respond that accountability, scores, and testing are a reason they entered the field of teaching. They don't get you out of bed in the morning. This activity shows that the focus in schools often strays from the meaningful and fulfilling aspects of education—from what most deeply impacts the goal of helping students succeed in life.

The intense focus on accountability and scores as motivators for investment has pulled teachers further and further away from what called them to education. As Lyle Kirtman (2013) notes,

> Policymakers want a high sense of urgency for change and results in education in order to be competitive worldwide. However, the nature of the approach to prescribe accountability and to emphasize evaluation has the potential of decreasing the success rate of our schools. . . . Rules and regulations are important but not as motivators to achieve great results for students and staff. (p. 15)

To achieve systemic change, schools and districts must redirect their primary focus from test scores to their fundamental purpose, the reason they exist, the ideal school they seek to become, and the commitment required to create a bridge between today's vision and tomorrow's reality. Educators must undergo a major mental paradigm shift. Schools will not get "top downed" into better performance; we must invest our focus, time, energy, and resources in what matters most to educators.

This is not to suggest that schools and systems do away with accountability, testing, and scores. Results are important, and a focus on results is the third big idea of a PLC; however, they must stay in proper context with the first two big ideas: (1) a focus on learning and (2) building a collaborative culture (DuFour, DuFour, Eaker, & Many, 2010a). Accountability, testing, and scores are a product of a school's primary focus on learning.

We seek to guide you in redirecting your focus so you can meet accountability goals by investing your available time, energy, and resources into achieving your shared mission. Becoming your ideal school begins with examining your culture, fundamental purpose, and commitment to ensuring learning for all. Implementing your PLC in a way that will result in sustained improvement requires a culture of collective responsibility.

Building Shared Commitment

Building shared commitment to collective responsibility requires time to reflect and explore together. We cannot emphasize enough how important it is to invest time in exploring the questions we present in this book. Traditional school culture doesn't encourage staff members to engage in collective reflection. But as Albert Einstein cautioned, you cannot solve your problems with the same thinking you used to create them. You must usher in new thinking, and connect with what really motivates and inspires educators to do and be their best.

According to Jon Katzenbach and Douglas Smith (1993), "The essence of a team is shared commitment. Without it, groups perform as individuals; with it, they become a powerful unit of collective performance . . . teams develop direction, momentum and commitment by working to shape a meaningful purpose" (p. 112). This wisdom is a tried-and-true principle of collective mobilization.

The idea that commitment is the essence of teamwork is widely accepted in business, sports, and a variety of other sectors, but in education, this essential element of school improvement receives only cursory attention. For our purposes in this book, commitment means the entire school examines, explores, and embraces collective responsibility.

Collective responsibility is necessary for a PLC to be successful. Staff members must adopt two conditions as the foundation for the shared mission of the school.

1. We believe that all students can learn at high levels.

2. We make the collective commitment to ensure learning occurs for every student.

This collective commitment guides all actions at your school, serving as your school's North Star. With a myriad of issues competing for the attention of educators, these two conditions also remind you to always come back to your mission: why do you exist? Collective responsibility means much more than clichés, slogans, and catchphrases. It requires that the moral imperative (the why of your work) be embedded in every aspect of your school's culture—through every decision, behavior, and action taken as a school.

Believing That All Students Can Learn at High Levels

Let's clarify what we mean when we say all students can learn at high levels. We agree with the definition provided by Austin Buffum, Mike Mattos, and Chris Weber (2012): "'high school plus,' meaning every student will graduate from high school with the skills and knowledge required to continue to learn" (p. 16). High school plus can take on a variety of forms. It can include owning a business, establishing a trade, college, internships, and other opportunities. One very sobering fact is that students who don't learn beyond high school live shorter, less healthy lives and make less money than students whose learning continues past high school (Bureau of Labor

Statistics, 2013). As Craig D. Jerald (2009) states in Defining a 21st Century Education:

> The demand for educated workers will continue to be high, and those who obtain postsecondary education or training can continue to expect to earn a premium while those who do not will have far fewer opportunities to earn a living wage. (p. 30)

In our consulting work with schools, we ask educators if they believe all students can learn *at high levels* (high school plus). Recall the first question we ask participants to examine—Why did you become an educator?—and how it garners universal agreement. This second question about high levels of learning, however, typically prompts universal disagreement. Convictions begin to give way to conditions. Staff members move from the conviction of believing all students can learn to the conditions attached to the belief. These conditions usually begin with the word *if*. See if any of the following conditions sound familiar.

We believe all students can learn at high levels if:

- They come from homes with lots of support and involved parents
- They are well behaved, respectful, and compliant
- They speak the language
- They come from one side of town versus the other side of town
- They are of a certain race
- They aren't Title I or on free or reduced lunch
- They have no identified learning disabilities

Labels often begin as identifiers of how people are *incidentally* different. Over time, however, labels begin to represent more than identification and support. Labels begin to damage those they identify and lower expectations. Jackson (2011) refers to this as *control through classification*, the prejudgmental practice of sorting students based on standardized criteria. Marginalizing labels often foster misperceptions about students, in turn perpetuating a cycle of prejudicing beliefs and lowering expectations, as evidenced by the staff responses to whether or not students can learn at high levels.

However, in education, as Buffum, Mattos, and Weber (2012) note, we know that all students can learn when provided with effective teaching—almost four decades of effective schools research from Ron Edmonds, Larry Lezotte, Wilbur Brookover, Michael Rutter, and others support this fact. In *What Works in Schools*, Robert J. Marzano (2003) states, "An analysis of research conducted over a thirty-five-year period demonstrates that highly effective schools produce results that almost entirely overcome the effects of student background" (p. 7). However, in spite of this overwhelming evidence, some schools continue to act on ineffective school beliefs (Buffum et al., 2012).

The research and evidence support the fact that schools make the difference—not where students are from; what they look like; their race, culture, or language; and who their parents are or aren't. What matters is what you do in school from the time students arrive until the time they leave. Despite this compelling case, here you are, in the 21st century, still at the mercy of factors outside your sphere of influence to determine your school's culture, achievement, expectations, and destiny.

The need for a paradigm shift is easy to understand, but clearly a challenge to implement and embed. Anthony Muhammad (2009) agrees that cultural change is a difficult form of change to accomplish:

> It takes knowledge of where a school has been and agreement about where the school should go to transform culture. It requires an ability to deal with beliefs, policies, and institutions that have buffered educators from change and accountability. It is a tightrope-walking act of major proportion. (p. 16)

In the end, the cultural change involved when shifting to a belief that all students can learn and taking responsibility for that learning requires considerable effort. When students and adults alike enjoy peace of mind about school and predictability of expectations, they can flourish (Williams, 2012).

Ensuring That All Students Learn at High Levels

A commitment to ensure student learning is the center of professional learning, decision making, and action in a PLC. It is the heart of the teaching-learning cycle. When educators take ownership of this commitment, learning (not teaching) becomes the focal point, creating positive student outcomes. When the belief is inherent that all students will learn, making excuses based on circumstances beyond the control of the school becomes unacceptable. Teachers replace these excuses with an understanding of variable student circumstances, and their planning takes these variables into consideration.

Members of PLCs constantly ask themselves, "What happens in our school when, despite our best efforts, a student does not learn?" (DuFour, DuFour, Eaker, & Karhanek, 2004, p. 7). It becomes the responsibility of PLCs to provide students with opportunities for intervention and establish systematic and timely supports. Ensuring that all students learn means fair and equitable instruction from classroom to classroom.

Educators in PLCs make collective commitments clarifying what each staff member will do to create a learning environment in which all students learn, and they use the evidence gathered from assessments to set results-oriented goals and monitor student progress. There is no waffling on the collective commitment to learning. Rather than operating as if their primary purpose were to ensure students are taught, these educators shift their focus to ensuring that all students learn essential knowledge, skills, and dispositions.

Making the collective commitment to ensure learning for every student can be an overwhelming responsibility. But what's the alternative? Are we willing to determine an acceptable percentage of students who fail? To that end, are we willing to print class rosters and highlight the names of students we believe will fail before any attempt at teaching and learning begins? Are we able, with any degree of certainty, to declare that some students are not worth the time, energy, and commitment that highly skilled adults can employ to effect change?

In our combined fifty years of educational service to students, we have not yet encountered a student who was beyond the reach of educators committed to being difference makers. It really does come back to the culture we collectively create and commit to at school. Does your school culture lend itself to a competition where ranking and sorting prevail, where you look to see who is better than whom? Or does your culture thrive on collaboration—a collective commitment that vows, "Let's be better for each other and for our students!"

About This Book

In this book, we present a four-stage model to take you through a framework we call *authentic alignment*. The four stages are as follows.

1. Exploring: The Why
2. Envisioning: The Eye
3. Connecting: The How
4. Integrating: The Now

You should notice a pattern between the four stages of authentic alignment and the four foundational pillars of a PLC as presented by DuFour, DuFour, and Eaker (2008) in their groundbreaking work.

1. Mission
2. Vision
3. Values
4. Goals

In their book *Revisiting Professional Learning Communities at Work*, DuFour, DuFour, and Eaker (2008) describe the four pillars, or foundations, of a PLC:

The very essence of a learning community is a focus on and a commitment to the learning of each student. When a school or district functions as a PLC, educators embrace high levels of learning for all students as both the reason the organization exists and the fundamental responsibility of those who work within it. To achieve the shared purpose, the members of a PLC create and are guided by a clear and compelling vision of what their schools and districts must become to help all students learn. They make collective commitments to clarify what each member will do to contribute to creating such organizations, and to use results-oriented goals for marking progress. This foundation of shared mission (purpose), vision (clear direction), values (collective commitments), and goals (indicators, timelines, and targets) not only addresses how educators will work to improve their schools, but also reinforces the moral purpose and collective responsibility that clarify why their day-to-day work is so important. (p. 15)

During our work with educators it has become clear to us that schools often lose sight of this foundation. Even though educators are working hard and going above and beyond on a daily basis, the impact of their efforts falls short of its great potential because building the pillars becomes more like a checklist of activities to be completed rather than the creation of a culture of learning for all that everyone must continually build, nurture, and sustain.

Often, schools address these four pillars during preplanning days or an annual leadership retreat and do not consider them again until the end of the school year. Authentic alignment helps schools soundly embed the four pillars of a PLC within a culture of collective responsibility so that PLC implementation doesn't stall. Through this process, we seek to help your PLC strengthen each pillar.

We begin in chapter 1 with a discussion about effective leadership in a PLC and the steps to create an effective leadership team, or guiding coalition, which is necessary to maximize learning in a school. Chapter 2 describes the four-stage authentic alignment process, including questions, indicators, strategies, and obstacles you may face as you lay the foundation for PLC transformation.

Chapters 3 through 6 delve deeper into each stage. The Why allows you and your staff to collaboratively uncover or strengthen your mission, while the Eye strengthens your vision—an ideal of what your school can become. Subsequently, you will explore the How—the ways in which you can systemically embed your renewed focus and collective commitments in the current school structure. The Now represents what you must do in the present to protect your culture by preserving collective commitments, achieving recipricol accountability, and planning and prioritizing your work.

In chapter 7, we examine how schools can strategically use the power of communication and celebration to focus primarily on the culture of collective responsibility. Finally, the epilogue discusses the school leader's role in the authentic alignment process and how to commit to a cycle of continuous improvement to keep your PLC moving forward.

From Stalling to Soaring

Our work as education consultants has led us to appreciate the need to understand the path we take before moving forward, including the challenges and roadblocks we may face. That is the purpose of this book: to help school leaders, staff members, and other stakeholders in their path to becoming a PLC. We seek to support schools in actually living their fundamental purpose—learning for all—so that instead of "ready, set, stall . . . ," schools advance toward a culture of collective responsibility, positioning them to soar.

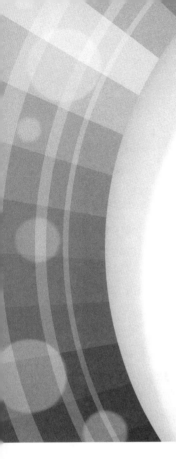

Chapter 1

Wanted: Leaders at Every Level

Leaders strike the match for schoolwide cultural change; staff fan the flames.

—KENNETH C. WILLIAMS

Our work with schools has illuminated one important point about what it takes to create schoolwide cultural change: leadership is not a solo act. A school's transition to a PLC requires leadership at all levels. A school leader can bring a topic to the forefront, frame a discussion, facilitate healthy, productive conflict, and provide the resources and support to move forward with the initiative. But school leaders alone cannot effect the sustained cultural change required to become a PLC. Everyone should take the opportunity to be a leader in a PLC at some point—whether formally or informally. Once the staff have built shared knowledge on how to create a school aligned with their core purpose and have established collective commitments to bring that school into being, then it becomes everyone's responsibility to protect and nurture the culture.

Early in his leadership career, Ken made the mistake of believing that his energy, enthusiasm, passion, and focus would be enough to turn the school he inherited around. It didn't take him long to realize that if he didn't change, he would be alone in his endeavor. Over time, he began to see that it was the staff members' encouragement to each other to commit to and deeply invest in the transformation that fanned the flames of their PLC. This investment shows that a culture is changing and moving in the right direction. Every single person in your organization has the potential to influence others. Sometimes this influence is overt, and other times it's subtle. People are leaders when they decide to become leaders and receive the opportunity to lead. The architects of the PLC model, DuFour, DuFour, and Eaker, emphasize the importance of building effective leadership at all levels in a PLC (DuFour et al., 2008, 2010a).

So before you begin to explore the four steps of authentic alignment, it is critical to examine the importance of a guiding coalition in a PLC. The guiding coalition is necessary to keep your culture focused on your mission, vision, and collective commitments. Your guiding coalition works interdependently to meet or exceed your established goals. Team members hold one another accountable for results and are able to act independently, aligned with your shared commitments. The first step in developing leadership at all levels is to assemble your guiding coalition.

Building an Effective Guiding Coalition

Whatever you call your team—guiding coalition, leadership team, or something else—the name is less important than its function in creating and sustaining a culture of collective responsibility. Typically comprising representatives from each collaborative teacher team, the administration, and classified and support staff, this team's primary responsibility is to unite and coordinate the school's collective efforts across grade levels, departments, and subjects.

DuFour et al. (2008) define a *guiding coalition* as "an alliance of key members of an organization who are specifically charged to lead a change process through the predictable turmoil" (p. 467).

According to them, members of the alliance should have shared objectives and high levels of trust. In order to move your school's culture in the direction of collective responsibility, the team must help guide the process to keep emphasis on shared leadership, ownership, and investment. Buffum et al. (2012) note,

> The composition of the team is critical. Every school has key individuals who have influence on campus. To give the coalition credibility, these individuals must be included, keeping in mind that some of your influential staff members may be individuals who may traditionally resist change. The coalition should also represent all relevant points of view and campus expertise. (p. 20)

In education, we do a poor job of identifying, nurturing, and dispersing leadership, especially when it comes to leadership teams. We see no shortage of leadership teams in schools. But commonly the *leadership* part rings hollow. When we ask school and teacher leaders how they developed their leadership teams, the answers often come down to leadership by default. Here are a few scenarios.

- "We have a grade-level team of three teachers, Jerry, Linda, and Joan. Joan is the representative from our team on the leadership team this year; Jerry fulfilled that role last year, so it is Linda's turn next."

- "Our leadership team representative receives a stipend to serve on the team. Therefore, we rotate the responsibility from year to year so everyone gets a chance to earn the extra money."

- "We let the principal decide who is on the team and then those people stay on the team until they decide they no longer want the position."

We have been treating leadership in our schools the same way for so long that we fail to step back and examine how it affects our culture. This is what we would like you to do now: take a step back and ask yourself if you're taking the proper care and getting the right people on the right teams in your school.

Creating Working Groups Versus Teams

Many leaders believe they have developed a leadership team when what they really have formed is a working group. Table 1.1 (Kirtman, 2013) shows the differences between a working group and a leadership team.

Table 1.1: Differences Between Working Groups and Leadership Teams

Working Groups	Leadership Teams
Have a strong, clearly focused leader	Have shared leadership roles
Have individual accountability	Value individual and mutual accountability
Have a purpose that is the same as the broader organization mission	Have a specific team purpose that the team itself delivers
Produce individual work and products	Produce collective work and products
Hold efficient meetings	Have open-ended discussion and encourage active problem solving
Effectiveness measured indirectly by their influence on others (such as financial performance of a business)	Performance measured directly by assessing collective work and products
Processes for accomplishing goals are discussion, decision, and delegation	Processes for accomplishing goals are discussion, decision, and sharing of actual work

Source: Kirtman, 2013, p. 35.

What do you notice about the differences between the working group and the leadership team? The differences Kirtman (2013) identifies support the definition of collaboration in a PLC established by DuFour et al. (2008): a group of people that works interdependently on a common goal for which they are held mutually accountable. So, in addition to ensuring the right people are on the leadership team, leaders must guarantee clarity of team function, purpose, and processes. Assembling the right people only for them to function as a working group as opposed to a team significantly diminishes their potential. Over time it impairs the development of a culture of collective responsibility at your school.

Assessing Your Guiding Coalition

Shifting your working group to a guiding coalition requires several paradigm shifts. Use the following inventory (figure 1.1, page 22) to assess where your team is on the continuum from working team to leadership team.

First complete the inventory on your own, honestly reflecting on each question. Cite evidence to support your position. Then share responses to the inventory as a group. Pay attention to both similarities and differences in the ratings of group members. Be sure to include your supporting evidence, even when teammates are in agreement.

Going From Efficiency to Advocacy

It's common to look at your team and conclude that there is little new learning to acquire. This is a mistake. We urge you to pay particular attention to the very tangible differences between a working group and leadership team at a school functioning as a PLC. Here are some important shifts to keep in mind.

1. Our team has shared leadership roles.

Not True of Our Team   True of Our Team

        1   2   3   4   5   6   7

2. Our team values individual and mutual accountability.

Not True of Our Team   True of Our Team

        1   2   3   4   5   6   7

3. Our team has a specific team purpose that the team itself delivers.

Not True of Our Team   True of Our Team

        1   2   3   4   5   6   7

4. Our team produces collective work and products.

Not True of Our Team   True of Our Team

        1   2   3   4   5   6   7

5. Our team has open-ended discussions and encourages active problem solving.

Not True of Our Team   True of Our Team

        1   2   3   4   5   6   7

6. Our team performance is measured directly by assessing collective work and products.

Not True of Our Team   True of Our Team

        1   2   3   4   5   6   7

7. Our processes for accomplishing goals are discussion, decision, and sharing of actual work.

Not True of Our Team   True of Our Team

        1   2   3   4   5   6   7

8. I believe our next best three steps to become a leadership team or guiding coalition are:

_____

_____

_____

Figure 1.1: Leadership team inventory.

*Visit **go.solution-tree.com/plcbooks** for a reproducible version of this figure.*

The Shift From Representative to Team Member

Traditional teams often include staff members who attend as representatives of their job-alike teams. Each representative attends with the best interests of his or her particular team in mind.

While members of a guiding coalition should appear on behalf of stakeholder groups throughout the school, their function is not to represent the best interest of their respective job-alike teams. The guiding coalition is a team in and of itself, which has agreed on its own shared purpose, team goals, and collective commitments.

The Shift From Messenger to Missionary

The role of the team member in a traditional school primarily includes gathering information from either the principal or whoever is designated to present at the meeting. He or she then reports back to the job-alike team. Team members have the latitude to express support or disagree with information or decisions. It's not uncommon for a team member to claim, "I'm just the messenger."

In a guiding coalition, members develop goals and make decisions through the process of building shared knowledge and consensus. Instead of simply reporting back, members advocate for decisions made as a team. Members of a guiding coalition are active stakeholders, sharing in the decision making and then returning to their job-alike teams to champion the cause. In our training, we remind guiding coalition team members to live by this creed: we own what we decide.

These two shifts, along with Kirtman's (2013) distinctions between working groups and leadership teams, should help both teachers and school leaders understand the skills and competencies needed to be a member of a guiding coalition. Leadership by default can no longer be an acceptable means of selecting team members. In an effort to support teachers and administrators in shaping a guiding coalition, we outline some of the high-leverage, research-based competencies present in members of successful teams.

Competencies of Guiding Coalition Members

As we move away from the model of leadership by default to concentrate on attracting and persuading the right people to be a part of the guiding coalition, it's important to offer some criteria. We advocate using Kirtman's (2013) seven leadership competencies as a lens through which to consider not only the strengths of people you want to attract to the team, but also as a catalyst to process and improve individual leadership. Unless you use a computer to make selections based on objective criteria, there's always going to be a level of subjectivity in this process. We support that kind of face-to-face subjectivity. We value instinct, experience, and hunches. However, we find value in combining subjective elements with research-based objective measures that can contribute to the process. Objective measures are not yet widely used in education, but we believe this trend is changing.

Kirtman (2013) defines *competency* as "an observable behavior that demonstrates skills, learning, and experience" (p. 5). His seven leadership competencies are more than just a list of commonly known characteristics derived from the myriad of personal or leadership development texts on the market. We are not minimizing the credibility of these books, but Kirtman's work attracted us because his competencies for leaders are based on his work with over three hundred school districts and more than one thousand educational leaders. The competencies represent observations of effective leaders and the results of data analysis of over six hundred educational leaders on a series of highly validated and reliable leadership inventories. In addition, they integrate leadership competencies from other sectors, including health care, business, government, nonprofit organizations, and the military. These competencies are derived from research-based data gathered from vast field experience and that have been field tested with over seven hundred organizations covering a span of thirty years (Kirtman, 2013).

Guiding coalitions need these competencies to meet the 21st century challenges of shifting the existing paradigm—redirecting the primary focus from accountability, scores, and testing to the school's fundamental purpose and shared mission, vision, and commitments. This task is both doable and potentially daunting, and what it means for student and adult learning makes the challenge more than worthwhile. Kirtman has identified seven competencies for high-performing leaders in education, with accompanying subsets that can help them focus their professional development. Based on our experience in leading schools through the process of becoming PLCs, we find seamless alignment and direct application with six of Kirtman's seven competencies, so we have chosen to focus on the first six. Kirtman (2013) identifies the following characteristics as competencies for high-performing leaders.

1. Challenges the status quo
2. Builds trust through clear communications and expectations
3. Creates a commonly owned plan for success
4. Focuses on team over self
5. Has a high sense of urgency for change and sustainable results
6. Commits to continuous self-improvement
7. Builds external networks and partnerships

Challenges the Status Quo

High performers characteristically have less focus than others on rule following and compliance. This does not mean that high-performing leaders break rules. It does mean that they start with a primary focus on the shared mission, vision, commitments, and the results they want to achieve. They concentrate on helping teammates face the same direction and modeling mutual accountability for shared commitments. They tend to challenge current practices that are not in support of goals developed for improving student achievement. They are willing to take risks to achieve results. They are often courageous leaders pursuing the best for all students. Leaders with this characteristic:

- Challenge common practices and traditions that block improvements
- Are willing to take risks
- Look for innovations to get results
- Do not let rules and regulations block results and slow down action

Builds Trust Through Clear Communications and Expectations

This competency focuses on a leader's ability to influence and motivate others through clear communications and expectations. Trust is very important to these leaders because they tend to value effective collaboration and developing confidence with their teammates to achieve results. They are both competent and dependable. High performers are usually comfortable dealing with conflict, invite productive conflict, and are able to build trust with people who do not always agree with their ideas. Leaders with this characteristic:

- Are direct and honest about team commitments and obligations
- Invite productive conflict as a means to maximize productivity and problem solving
- Follow through with actions and on all commitments
- Ensure a clear understanding of written and verbal communications
- Are comfortable dealing with destructive conflict

Creates a Commonly Owned Plan for Success

Effective leaders tend to develop a systemically focused, written plan for success, which they strongly lead from and encourage their teams to invest in implementing. High performers are able to develop clear measurements for success and use the data to inform next steps. Leaders with this characteristic:

- Support the creation of written plans with the input of stakeholders and teammates
- Advocate for teammates investing in the plan
- Clarify agreed-on behavioral commitments associated with the plan
- Facilitate the collaborative team in adjusting the plan based on new data and changes
- Collaborate to develop clear measurements for each goal in the plan

Focuses on Team Over Self

High-performing leaders know that they cannot get results by themselves or expect to own all the best ideas. A leader is only as good as the strengths of the people around him or her, so effective leaders surround themselves with those who can strongly contribute to both guiding coalitions and collaborative teams. These leaders tend to give credit to their teams instead of highlighting individual performance. They understand the power of collective expertise, as opposed to traditional teacher isolation. High performers are able to put their egos aside for the sake of their teams' development and essential student results. Leaders with this characteristic:

- Commit to the ongoing development of the guiding coalition and their own collaborative teams
- Build a collaborative culture
- Seek constructive feedback
- Provide both praiseworthy and constructive feedback aligned with the shared mission
- Support the professional development of the guiding coalition and the collaborative team

Has a High Sense of Urgency for Change and Sustainable Results

A common element among high-performing leaders is their high sense of urgency for results. They nurture this sense of urgency in all stakeholders by focusing on the shared purpose as a means to improve results and ensuring that this moral imperative informs every expectation and product. Such leaders want action and fast movement on key issues and tend to quickly solve problems. They make tough decisions to help students rather than fall prey to the pressure of prioritizing adult comfort. Successful leaders also use instructional data in the change process. Leaders with this characteristic:

- Can be very decisive
- Use student learning results to inform necessary instructional change
- Support schoolwide use of high-leverage practices to ensure sustainable change
- Stay focused on the direction for the guiding coalition and their collaborative teams
- Are able to expect and manage change effectively

Commits to Continuous Self-Improvement

High-performing leaders constantly try to improve and satisfy curiosity about new ideas and practices. They learn from colleagues and stay open to criticism and honest feedback. These leaders recognize leadership as a journey filled with opportunities for improvement. Within their collaborative teams, they understand the value of using data to inform their practice and willingly compare data with teammates. High performers focus on improvement and results through the lens of the shared mission. Leaders with this characteristic:

- Have a high sense of curiosity for new practices to improve results

- Possess a willingness to change current practices for themselves and others, based on data
- Work collaboratively with teammates when considering changes to practices to obtain results
- Take responsibility for their own actions—no excuses—and model this at the team level as well
- Keep teammates focused on factors within their sphere of influence
- Have strong self-management and self-reflection skills

High-performing leaders may not excel in all of these competencies; however, they do exhibit strong skills and practices in almost all of them. All strong leaders understand that they must continually improve, and they realize that they can never master all these competencies as contexts change and practices evolve.

Building Your Guiding Coalition

Now that you have a list of powerful research-based competencies to consider, it's time to either create the guiding coalition or re-evaluate your existing leadership team. If you are a principal or school leader, you might be thinking about which members to select. If you are a teacher leader or support team leader, then you may be reflecting on your strengths and opportunities for growth as a member of the guiding coalition.

We can't emphasize enough that PLC leadership within a culture of collective responsibility is not a solo act. Recall the opening quote of this chapter. It states that while the principal is the spark for schoolwide cultural change, staff fan the flames. Cultural change spreads powerfully and widely when members of the guiding coalition champion the shared mission, vision, and collective commitments. In the early stages of building a culture of collective responsibility, the school leader must assemble the leadership team, and then make a compelling case for the changes required to develop a culture of collective responsibility. If the principal can't persuade a small group of influential teacher leaders to champion this culture, then he or she has no chance of helping the entire staff face the right direction.

Rather than simply listing the names of staff members you'd like to consider as part of the school's guiding coalition or leadership team, we would like you to first consider this: *leadership is influence.* In addition to the competencies we discussed in the previous section, it's important that the members of your leadership team are, in fact, influential. By *influential,* we mean that staff members respect them.

Do you know which colleagues your staff members respect most? We ask this question because school leaders rarely consider it. As leaders, we typically gravitate toward those who think like we do, are willing to go above and beyond, or are inclined to challenge ideas tactfully.

For example, you may be tempted to list people who are so in sync with your leadership style and vision that they jump on board with your ideas quickly and energetically. They are your most ardent supporters, and you can absolutely count on them to give anything you suggest a try. They sound like ideal candidates, right? Well, hold on; they, in fact, may be some of the *last* people you persuade to be a part of the school's guiding coalition. You'll want to consider the following research from the authors of *Influencer: The Power to Change Anything* (Patterson, Grenny, Maxfield, McMillan, & Switzler, 2008).

The first people to latch on to a new idea are unlike the masses in many ways. Kerry Patterson and his coauthors call these people *innovators.* They tend to be open to new ideas and smarter than average; however, Patterson et al. (2008) point out that "the key to getting the majority of any population to adopt a vital behavior is to find out who these innovators are *and avoid them like the plague.* If they embrace your new idea, it will surely die." This may seem unbelievable, and, in fact, we thought so when we first read it. But these people tend to always jump on board—regardless of the quality of an idea—and their colleagues know this. You want people on your guiding coalition who will influence others. It's incorrect to assume that those who influence are the same as those who are first out of the gate with implementation. When developing the guiding coalition at a school, you shouldn't include only people with whom you find it easy to work. Teams need critical thinkers and visionary thinkers as well.

Patterson et al. (2008) identify the second group to try an innovation as *early adopters*. They explain,

> Many early adopters are what are commonly known as *opinion leaders*. . . . They are different from innovators in one critical respect: They are socially *connected* and *respected*, and here's the real influence key: the rest of the population—over 85 percent—will not adopt the new practices until opinion leaders do. (p. 225)

Consider the following example. In the late 1970s and early 1980s, the financial investment brokerage firm E. F. Hutton launched a very successful marketing campaign. The campaign took the form of television commercials in which two people were in a crowded area such as an airport, the park, walking along the street, or the golf course. The two people having a private conversation are seen discussing personal financial matters. The first person shares information about an investment he or she is considering. For example, the first person might say, "My broker believes this company is going to be a great stock pick for the coming year. What does your broker say?" The second person says, "My broker is E. F. Hutton, and E. F. Hutton says . . ." and before he or she can say another word, the area falls completely silent and every person within earshot strains to hear the advice from the E. F. Hutton broker. At that moment, a voiceover intones, "When E. F. Hutton talks, people listen."

We have taken the E. F. Hutton slogan and applied it to the process of identifying your school's opinion leaders. Who are the E. F. Huttons at your school? Those who everyone stops and listens to when they have something to say?

Part I: Brainstorming Your E. F. Huttons and Evaluating Influencer Competency

Consider which members of your staff meet the following criteria.

- They are smart.
- They tend to be open to new ideas.
- They are socially *connected* and *respected.*
- When they *talk*, people *listen.*
- When they *act*, people *follow.*
- No one will adopt new practices until the opinion leader does.

Now take a few moments for a quick brainstorm. Who are the staff members who come to mind immediately as your E. F. Huttons? Make a list of the staff members who fit the criterion of, "When _____ talks, people listen."

Next, indicate each individual's level of influence using the following scale:

- 1—Minimal influence
- 2—Slightly influential
- 3—Somewhat influential
- 4—Very influential
- 5—Extremely influential

Next we will guide you through using a more focused lens to inform your consideration and selection.

Part II: Reviewing the Leadership Competencies

Now review each of the competencies and their characteristics (adapted from Kirtman, 2013).

1. Challenges the status quo
   - Challenges common practices and traditions if they block improvements
   - Is willing to take risks
   - Looks for innovations to get results
   - Does not let rules and regulations block results and slow down action
2. Builds trust through clear communications and expectations
   - Is direct and honest about team commitments and obligations
   - Invites productive conflict as a means to maximize productivity and problem solving
   - Follows through with actions and on all commitments
   - Ensures a clear understanding of written and verbal communications
   - Is comfortable dealing with destructive conflict
3. Creates a commonly owned plan for success
   - Supports the creation of written plans with input of stakeholders and teammates
   - Advocates for teammates investing in the plan
   - Clarifies agreed-upon behavioral commitments associated with the plan
   - Facilitates the collaborative team in adjusting the plan based on new data and changes
   - Collaborates to develop clear measurements for each goal in the plan
4. Focuses on team over self
   - Commits to the ongoing development of the guiding coalition and his or her own collaborative team
   - Builds a collaborative culture
   - Seeks constructive feedback
   - Provides both praiseworthy and constructive feedback aligned with the shared mission

- Supports the professional development of the guiding coalition and the collaborative team

5. Has a high sense of urgency for change and sustainable results

  - Can be very decisive
  - Uses student learning results to inform needed instructional change
  - Supports schoolwide use of high-leverage practices to ensure sustainability of change
  - Stays focused on the direction of the guiding coalition and his or her collaborative team
  - Is able to expect and manage change effectively

6. Commits to continuous self-improvement

  - Has a high sense of curiosity for new practices to improve results
  - Possesses a willingness to change current practices for him- or herself and others, based on data
  - Works collaboratively with teammates when considering changing practices to obtain results
  - Takes responsibility for his or her own actions—no excuses—and models this at the team level as well
  - Keeps teammates focused on factors within his or her sphere of influence
  - Has strong self-management and self-reflection skills

Part III: Evaluating Based on the Leadership Competencies

Look back to your list of the E. F. Huttons with the competencies you just reviewed in mind. Using figure 1.2, evaluate potential team members through the lens of each competency and indicate your evaluation of their strength in each area using the code provided. Make anecdotal notes as needed.

Name of Staff Member _____

	Competency	Code	Notes
1	Challenges the status quo		
2	Builds trust through clear communications and expectations		
3	Creates a commonly owned plan for success		
4	Focuses on team over self		
5	Has a high sense of urgency for change and sustainable results		
6	Commits to continuous self-improvement		

Code Key: N = Not a strength; S = Slight strength; M = Moderate strength; E = Exceptional strength

Note: High-performance leaders do not excel in all of these competencies. However, they do exhibit strong skills and practices in almost all of the competencies. All strong leaders understand that they must continually improve, and they realize that they can never master all these competencies.

Figure 1.2: Leadership competencies evaluation tool.

Visit go.solution-tree.com/plcbooks for a reproducible version of this figure.

Note that there's an important difference between a competent leader and an influencer. A person can possess several of the leadership qualities listed in the previous step and yet lack the social connections and respect that would signal a true influencer. Staff members selected for the guiding coalition must possess both. They need leadership competencies to be successful leaders, and they must be influencers to effectively advocate for change, support collective commitments, and champion the shared mission (in other words, fan the flames).

Part IV: Narrowing Choices and Making Decisions

By now, you and your team (if you're using a team to make leadership decisions) have gathered good, solid information to go along with your gut feelings, hunches, and observations. You're ready to use these resources to make more informed decisions about collaborative teams. Note that we recommend that a member of each teacher team be on the guiding coalition. You may need to make some tough choices. Have the courage to do so. You now have data that might reveal a staff member is a great educator, but not someone who should be a part of the school's guiding coalition. Eliminate any person from your list who doesn't possess strengths in most of the six competencies and those with little influence. Does your team have the necessary balance?

Making Leadership Transformational

We have clarity on the difference between a traditional leadership team and one in a PLC. We have also outlined the high-leverage competencies necessary for members of the guiding coalition as well as activities to help select them. Now we'll examine the overarching role of a PLC guiding coalition. Buffum et al. (2012) caution that the guiding coalition is not the school "dictatorship" committee but a team that learns deeply about best practices, assesses candidly the school's current reality, determines potential next steps to improve the school, identifies possible obstacles and points of leverage, and plans the best way to create staff consensus and ownership. To accomplish this, your team must meet frequently, especially at the beginning of the process of building a culture of collective responsibility. You must charge your members with championing and promoting the initiative. Their duty is to lead the process, not take a top-down approach.

Building a culture of collective responsibility is challenging work. It requires a focus on what Anthony Muhammad (2009) calls *technical change* and *cultural change*:

> [Technical changes are] changes to the tools or mechanisms professionals use to do their jobs effectively. These changes within a school context refer to changes in structure, policies, or teaching tools (for example, changing from a six-period school day to a block schedule, revising the curriculum with changes in learning standards or text material, or offering more advanced and rigorous classes, to name a few). . . . [Cultural change is] knowledge of where a school has been, and agreement about where the school should go, requiring an ability to deal with beliefs, policies, and institutions. (p. 16)

Cultural change in a PLC requires a close examination of habits, assumptions, and beliefs. Muhammad (2009) refers to this process as transformative. That is the new paradigm for leadership teams. Their role is, in essence, transformational leadership at every level. Kirtman (2013) references how the role of the school leader has evolved; it is no longer transactional but transformational. The transactional role involves the day-to-day interactions between people to exchange information, data, and materials; you need information, and another person provides what you need. A transformational role involves focusing on common goals and aspirations to effect fundamental change and improvement (Kirtman, 2013). We advocate this type of role for the work of the school leader and guiding coalition. It no longer suffices to send a representative to meet with the principal every two weeks who returns with memos and notes to disseminate. In a culture of collective responsibility, the team members' roles and responsibilities go far beyond simply sharing information in a follow-up session. One of the first charges of the guiding coalition is to facilitate the process of creating consensus for a culture of collective responsibility.

Creating Consensus for a Culture of Collective Responsibility

An early primary responsibility of the guiding coalition is helping to identify aligned behaviors and practices to support the school's fundamental purpose. This doesn't happen via edict or memorandum. Creating consensus in a PLC starts with exploring and discussing several critical questions. The following process supports this discussion.

Remember that a culture of collective responsibility is based on two fundamental beliefs:

1. We, as educators, must accept responsibility to ensure high levels of learning for every student. While parental, societal, and economic forces impact student learning, the actions of educators will ultimately determine each student's success in school.

2. We believe all students can learn at high levels—high school plus—meaning every student will graduate from high school with the skills and knowledge required to continue to learn.

Discussing the following questions will help a guiding coalition create consensus for a culture of collective responsibility aligned with these two beliefs. As a team, address each of the questions in four stages.

1. Reflect and record your honest and unfiltered response to each question individually.

2. Gather in small groups and share your individual responses. Reserve your response and judgment until everyone in your group has had an opportunity to share. Make note of points that jump out at you.

3. Discuss the responses and look for opportunities for next steps.

4. Come back together and share your most salient responses to each question with the entire guiding coalition.

Note that this process may require more than one session.

Questions for Consensus Building

Consider the following questions from Austin Buffum, Mike Mattos, and Chris Weber (2011, pp. 27–28) in their book *Simplifying Response to Intervention*:

1. **How will we provide a compelling case for change?** For someone to change, he or she first must see a compelling reason to change. Raising test scores or meeting district, state, or federal mandates hardly makes a compelling case. Instead, paint a picture of what adulthood could look like for students who don't succeed in school.

2. **What must we do differently?** Besides a compelling reason to change, we must also have a doable plan for change. The noblest cause is useless if staff members see the changes required as unrealistic. They want a clear picture of exactly what changes are necessary to achieve learning for all students.

3. **How do we know our changes will work?** Having experienced the pendulum of school change, educators are understandably skeptical of it. What evidence demonstrates the validity of the recommended changes? (For example, the website www.allthingsplc.info features dozens of schools and hundreds of pages of research validating the PLC and response to intervention [RTI] models.)

4. **What concerns do we expect, especially from staff members who often oppose change?** The guiding coalition should brainstorm to anticipate staff concerns regarding the recommended changes. What will the leadership's response to these concerns be?

5. **What is the best setting or structure for the conversations needed to create consensus?** One of the guiding coalition's greatest leverage points is its ability to determine the location, structure, and timing of the conversations to

create staff consensus. All stakeholders must have a voice in the process, but not necessarily in the same meeting. Sometimes the aggressive opinions of a loud, resistant minority can drown out the feelings of the silent majority. Consider a series of meetings with teams, grade levels, or departments. Also, set clear norms for the meetings; professional, respectful dialogue is essential.

6. **How will we know if we have reached consensus?** Remember, it does not take 100 percent approval to get started; it takes consensus. Consensus is reached when all stakeholders have had a say and the will of the group has emerged and is evident, even to those who most oppose it (DuFour et al., 2010a). Consider how many key people you will need to reach the tipping point necessary for consensus.

Achieving True Commitment

You may look at this process and the other processes outlined in this book and wonder if it's worth the time required to explore them. If you're interested in real investment and commitment from your school leaders and staff, then your answer should be *yes*. When questions arise, heed the advice offered by Buffum et al. (2012):

> In the end, true commitment comes when people see that the changes work. So the key is to build consensus, then get started doing the work. You will never get commitment until you start doing the work, but you cannot start until you get consensus. (p. 31)

In the next chapter, we introduce the authentic alignment model. It will help you intentionally reflect on and integrate your school's mission, vision, and collective commitments with the essential work of your PLC—to build a culture of collective responsibility and strengthen your PLC's foundational pillars. The four-stage process guides you through examining your school's culture and deciding which beliefs and practices are moving you toward your ideal school, and which ones are causing you to stray. For each stage, we outline some of the more important roles and functions of the guiding coalition, the school leader, and teacher leaders.

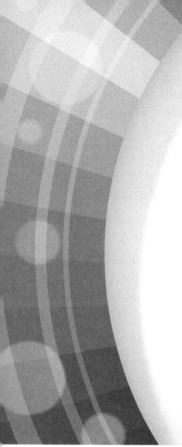

Chapter 2

What Is Authentic Alignment?

All organizations are perfectly aligned to get the results they get.

—ARTHUR W. JONES

As we explained in the introduction, the authentic alignment model is based on the four pillars of a PLC: mission, vision, values, and goals (DuFour et al., 2010a). According to DuFour, DuFour, Eaker, and Many (2010a), each pillar asks a different question of educators. Teachers and administrators work together to consider the questions and reach consensus regarding their collective positions on each question. In doing so, they build a solid foundation for their PLC and all subsequent work. As DuFour, DuFour, Eaker, and Many note (2010a), "If staff members have not considered the questions, have done so only superficially, or are unable to establish common ground regarding their positions on the questions, any and all future efforts to improve the school will stand on shaky ground" (p. 30). DuFour, DuFour, Eaker, and Many (2010a) describe the four pillars as follows.

- **Pillar One: Mission**—The mission pillar asks the question, "Why?" More specifically, it asks, "Why do we exist?" The intent of this question is to help reach agreement regarding the fundamental purpose of the school. This clarity of purpose can establish priorities and becomes an important factor in guiding decisions. (p. 30)

- **Pillar Two: Vision**—The vision pillar asks the question, "What?" That is, "What must we become in order to accomplish our fundamental purpose?" In pursuing this question, a staff attempts to create a compelling, attractive, realistic future that describes what they hope their school will become. Vision provides a sense of direction and the basis for assessing both the current reality of the school and potential strategies, programs, and procedures to improve upon that reality. (pp. 30–31)

- **Pillar Three: Values**—The values pillar clarifies collective commitments. . . . It asks, "How must we behave to create the school that will achieve our purpose?" In answering this question, educators shift from offering philosophical musings on mission or the shared hopes for the school of the future to making commitments to act in certain ways—starting today. Clarity on this topic guides the individual work of each member of the staff and outlines how each person can contribute to the improvement initiative. (p. 33)

- **Pillar Four: Goals**—The final pillar of the foundation asks members to clarify the specific goals they hope to achieve as a result of the improvement initiative. Those provide staff members with a sense of their short-term priorities and the steps to achieve the benchmarks.

Effective goals foster both the results orientation of a PLC and individual and collective accountability for achieving the results. Goals help close the gap between the current reality and where the staff hopes to take the school—the shared vision. (pp. 33, 36)

There is no ambiguity in these definitions, and DuFour, DuFour, Eaker, and Many (2010a) have done exceptional work to clarify any misunderstandings about PLCs. Despite this we have found that the elements of these four foundational pillars are not always executed with fidelity in all schools. When schools address the questions superficially, then their PLCs rest on shaky ground. The failure to build shared knowledge and consensus dooms even educators armed with the best intentions never to realize the benefits of becoming a PLC. We have often worked with schools and districts that treat examination of the questions associated with the four pillars as an activity to check off a list. The process of authentic alignment is a tool to help you deepen this examination, strengthening your PLC's foundation.

So, what is authentic alignment, and how does it help build a culture of collective responsibility to strengthen PLCs so they soar rather than stall? Take a moment and reflect on the attributes you associate with the word *alignment*. What comes to mind? When we ask educators to reflect on alignment, the connections they make tend to involve preparation and planning—a coordinated effort that results in successfully melding various parts of a system. When parts are aligned, the outcomes are more predictable, more efficiently attained, and more likely to be the desired result.

Now consider authenticity. *Authenticity* involves truthfulness, commitment, sincerity, and devotion. Considering authenticity brings to mind the origin or source—the core. Now consider the definition of *authenticity* in the context of collective responsibility. Consider the following questions:

- What is at the core of our daily work? In the context of our work, to what are we devoted?

- How often do we reflect on the core of our work, our commitments, and why we make them?

- As a school, what is our mission? Our purpose? Have we clarified them?

Authentic alignment helps connect *what* we do in schools with the *why*. When there's no connection between what we do and why we do it, the best a school can hope for is compliance. There may be investment in getting things done, but that doesn't guarantee a shared purpose that serves as a lens for the work, guiding decisions, actions, commitments, and behaviors. Your PLC will soar and flourish when it rests on the strong foundation of the four pillars, when the why of the work permeates every aspect of your learning community.

Authentic Alignment

The authentic alignment process involves four stages that will support your learning community as you move from compliance to commitment and from stalling to soaring. Each of the four stages includes opportunities for reflection to guide your work and practical strategies for establishing a culture of collective responsibility at your school.

With the authentic alignment process, PLCs:

- Explore their core beliefs and capture the essence of their shared mission

- Build shared knowledge about best practice while envisioning and creating a description of the school they seek to become

- Reconnect with the moral imperative of their collective commitment to the essential work of a PLC

- Systematically integrate the mission, vision, and collective commitments into existing school structures

The four stages of creating a culture of authentic alignment are:

1. Exploring: The Why
2. Envisioning: The Eye
3. Connecting: The How
4. Integrating: The Now

Table 2.1 shows the four stages of authentic alignment and the goal of each stage.

Table 2.1: The Four Stages of Authentic Alignment and Their Goals

Stage	Goal
Exploring: The Why	Schools *identify* their fundamental purpose and *develop* their guiding mantra.
Envisioning: The Eye	Schools *envision* and create a description of the school they seek to become.
Connecting: The How	Schools *connect* with the moral imperative of their *collective commitment* to the essential work of a PLC.
Integrating: The Now	Schools *systematically integrate* the mission, vision, and collective commitments into existing structures to reach their goals.

Staff members must align every decision, strategy, initiative, practice, intervention, expectation, and opportunity for enrichment with the shared mission. Instead of getting hung up on scores, testing, and accountability, their focus rests on achieving the shared mission and vision in order to create their ideal school. Authentic alignment helps you go beyond a ceremonial connection to the shared mission and vision; it's more than lip service.

As DuFour et al. (2008) note, becoming a PLC cannot be reduced to a recipe or a prescriptive set of activities. Your PLC is not something you *do*; it is something you *are* (DuFour et al., 2010a). Committing to the essential work of a PLC through the lens of your shared mission and vision arms you with the collective efficacy you need to live the promises of the posters on your walls, not simply hang them. The challenge schools face is to consider this idea of alignment and avoid simply assuming it's in place already. Before you delve more deeply into the authentic alignment framework, it's important to perceive and accept the entrenched 21st century paradigm of high-stakes testing and accountability and recognize how the focus must change.

Culture Eats Structure for Lunch

Consider all the new initiatives you have experienced in your school or district. You might have thought to yourself, "This too shall pass." Your school then began to implement all of the steps and strategies involved with the new initiative. In the beginning, you noticed compliance, but not investment. After a while, each initiative felt like one more chore to do, one more item on an overflowing plate. It felt like something done *to you*. Did you watch that initiative unfold only to see it die a systematic death—a passing that you could have predicted almost perfectly on a calendar? If you have experienced this, then you have seen what we call *culture eating structure for lunch*. When a PLC has not caught on with deep implementation, it often means that the school has focused too much on developing the structures of a PLC and not embraced the challenging, essential cultural changes.

The Four-Step Process

Authentic alignment works within the PLC culture to help you examine, explore, and embed PLC elements during the important initial stages of becoming a PLC. It also provides supports that deepen and enhance the vital work of establishing meaning and purpose, examining the existing culture, and using existing resources to help maintain PLC elements throughout the year. We say that authentic alignment helps you *slow down to speed up*, allowing you to take time to focus on what's important early in the process to save time later. It helps you reflect deeply on the initial stages of the PLC transformation process to bring more meaning, cohesiveness, and purpose to your collective work.

Authentic alignment is not an add-on, a replacement, or a substitute for any aspect of the PLC process. Rather, our work is like adding additional mortar for the foundation of a learning community. The steps are as follows.

Exploring: The Why

The first stage of authentic alignment is exploring (the Why). This stage strengthens the first foundational pillar of a PLC: mission. In this stage, we provide tools and protocols to help you *identify* your fundamental purpose and *develop* your guiding school mantra. A *mantra* is an energy-infused phrase, easy to remember and embed in daily work, which expresses the spirit of the mission statement. A mantra is akin to a motto, albeit more fundamental to a school's internal purpose than a simple slogan. It's concise, repeatable, and core to a school's existence. The mantra is easily understood, suitable to rally around, and represents the unwavering core values that drive your daily work. Your school's mantra answers fundamental questions such as these.

- What do we believe?
- What do we want to achieve?
- Why do we go to work each day?
- Why does our school exist?

We see the process of developing a guiding mantra as another way to reconnect to your mission and serve as a triggered reminder—

hearing the mantra will make your team immediately recall the mission. Traditional mission statements in non-PLC schools are often bloated with words, devoid of any passion, and, as a result, often forgotten immediately. They may seek through elaborate wordsmithing to be all things to all people. The questions a traditional mission statement seeks to answer are very important. The problem in most schools is that little about the mission statement survives the day it was developed.

To be clear: clarifying the shared mission of your PLC is critical. A school can't build a culture of collective responsibility unless staff members discuss the fundamental purpose of the school. The remaining steps of authentic alignment further expound the need to move beyond treating the mission statement as some sort of checklist activity and, instead, letting it drive the actions of all members of the school community.

Envisioning: The Eye

The second stage of authentic alignment is envisioning (the Eye). This stage helps strengthen the second foundational pillar of a PLC: vision. In this stage, we help you *envision* and create a description of the school you seek to become. We have heard many people use the terms *vision* and *mission* interchangeably. In fact, they are quite different. Vision is located in the future, and mission is found in the present—what you value and believe right now. Once you are clear on your fundamental purpose and have created a picture of the school you seek to become, you have the fertile soil you need for collective responsibility to flourish. Anything short of this level of clarity results in random acts of improvement; no consistent, cohesive commitment to effective practice exists, meaning some staff members engage in it and others opt out. Envisioning moves your thinking two, three, or even five years into the future. You will describe an ideal *learning for all* school. You will communicate how it differs from your current culture, how it feels, what it looks like, and how it sounds. Envisioning contributes to strategic action planning because it lays the groundwork for a discussion of the requirements to build your future school. Since you must do more than hold hands and hope, the Eye stage provides an opportunity for staff members to build shared knowledge about best practices rooted in building a culture of collective responsibility. This shared knowledge is the foundation of the collective commitments made in the next stage of authentic alignment.

In her book *Leading With Trust*, Susan Stephenson (2009) advises,

> Vision scenarios are:
>
> - Passionate, optimistic, and inspirational
> - Hopes and dreams
> - Lighthouses where guiding stars show us the way
> - Magnets to pull us toward the future
> - Stories or pictures
>
> When we put our dreams into action, the results are powerful. Without a strong vision, we have no confidence that our actions will take us where we need to go. (p. 147)

Connecting: The How

The third stage of the authentic alignment model is connecting (the How). This stage helps strengthen the third foundational pillar of a PLC: values. This stage *connects* the moral imperative of your *collective commitment* to the important work of a PLC. As DuFour, DuFour, Eaker, and Many (2010a) explain, the essential work of a PLC involves:

1. Creating a collaborative culture
2. Clearly defining what every student needs to learn
3. Constantly measuring effectiveness
4. Systematically responding when students do and do not learn

We'll explore each of these four areas, provide tools for starting out, and pose guiding questions so you can assess the progress of your school or team on this essential work. Your school's best path to effective transformation into a PLC is not simply knowledge of how to take the necessary steps, but a simultaneous, deep collective commitment and connection to the Why of the work. If you are new to PLCs, then the connecting process of the How will help strengthen your efforts. If your school has already undergone the transformation into a PLC and you have embedded the essential work in your PLC structures, then this is a great opportunity to assess and adjust your efforts. This step helps schools that tend to gravitate toward the work itself first without paying the necessary attention to the Why of the work. It fulfills the critical need to build shared knowledge about the most promising practices for improving schools.

Integrating: The Now

The final stage of authentic alignment is integrating (the Now). This stage helps strengthen the fourth foundational pillar of your PLC: goals. This is where you *systematically integrate* mantra (your Why work), vision (your Eye work), and commitments (your How work) into your existing structures, into the fabric of your everyday life at school. As the authentic alignment model comes full circle, consistently keeping the primary focus centered has proven to be a challenge in many of the schools we've encountered. The temptation is ever present to slip back into the paradigm of accountability, scores, and testing. You must stay mindful of the challenge to systematically integrate critical foundational work into everything you do. The question you must keep in mind is, How do we integrate our purpose, vision, and commitments so pervasively that they become a lens through which everything is done at our school? This desired goal is not new to schools, but successful execution is all too uncommon. We provide tools to help schools address important questions such as:

- How will we organize people into teams to support collaboration?
- How will we provide time for collaboration?
- How will we create a guaranteed and viable curriculum (DuFour & Marzano, 2011)?
- How will we monitor each student's learning?
- How will we ensure that students who struggle receive additional time and support for learning that are timely, diagnostic, directive, and systematic?

Traditional schools seek to simply answer these questions, but rarely revisit them once they are answered. PLCs that have built a culture of collective responsibility realize that addressing these questions is a cyclical activity: the questions are explored, answered, revisited, and revised as appropriate. This ongoing cycle of inquiry is rooted in acknowledgment that no two students, classes, or educators are the same. What *is* the same is the mission: learning for all.

In addition to this cycle of inquiry, the goals in the Now stage are further embedded through the use of storytelling and celebration. Most schools have already embedded these aspects in their cultures. We find them to be great opportunities for schools to more deeply implement collective responsibility without adding to an already overflowing list of things to do.

Creating a Culture of Collective Responsibility

Figure 2.1 (page 52) provides a visual representation of the authentic alignment model. The Why in the middle signifies that a school's agreed-on fundamental purpose should permeate every aspect and every stage of becoming a PLC. The Why should remain at the forefront while you are:

- Committing to the clear vision of the school you seek to become (examined in the Eye)
- Engaging in the essential work of a PLC (examined in the How)

- Systematically keeping your fundamental purpose at the forefront of all decisions (examined in the Now)
- Engaging in cycles of inquiry (exploring, answering, revisiting, and revising) regarding specific cultural and structural questions:
  - Using storytelling to reinforce and support your purpose and as a vehicle to share breakthroughs to move toward the shared vision
  - Celebrating success connected to your fundamental purpose

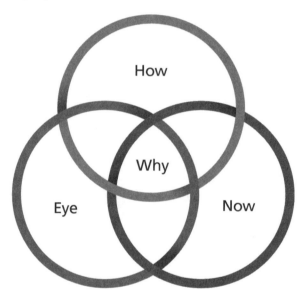

Figure 2.1: Creating a culture of collective responsibility.

DuFour et al. (2008) remind us that leaders do not change the culture to get people to act in new ways; they change how people act to change the culture (Kotter & Cohen, 2002, as cited in DuFour et al., 2008):

> It is essential to understand 1) the challenge of changing culture begins with the challenge of changing behavior,

and therefore 2) actual changes in culture occur late in the process. Schools and districts can initiate new practices and processes to promote a new culture, stimulate dialogue to articulate and re-examine existing assumptions, and build shared knowledge and create new experiences to foster different beliefs and assumptions, but the culture will not really be transformed until new practices, processes, assumptions, and beliefs become the new norms, the new "how we do things around here." (p. 108)

We have had the honor of working with hundreds of schools across North America as they improve learning by becoming PLCs. While there is no longer a debate about whether PLCs are a viable model to improve both student and adult learning, the fact is that many schools still struggle to see the fruits of their labor. A common challenge among struggling schools is building the cultural aspects of a PLC while implementing the structural elements. So how can schools engage in the actual day-to-day work of a PLC while also nurturing a PLC culture? This is the question that authentic alignment helps you answer.

From Compliance to Collective Responsibility

It can be difficult to tell the difference between compliance with and commitment to collective responsibility. How do you really know that your school is authentically aligned and not simply compliant? When your school operates in a culture of authentic alignment, the following are true.

- As part of the collaborative team, you're either getting better at your job or helping someone else get better.

- There are no excuses, just variables. Your teams focus on what you can control instead of what you can't, that is, outside factors such as issues at home, parental support, socioeconomic challenges, and language.

- You and everyone on your staff understand that every child is "your" child, and the failure of any one of them is not an option.

- PLCs are not something you *do*, but something you *are*.

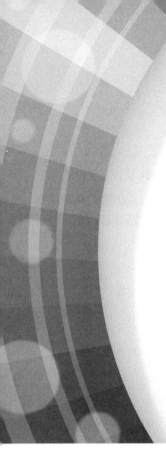

Chapter 3

Exploring: The Why

There are only two ways to influence human behavior: you can manipulate it or you can inspire it.

—SIMON SINEK

Exploring, or the Why, is the process of examining your fundamental purpose and core beliefs. Your goal is to capture the essence of your school's mission in a guiding mantra to help strengthen that mission, the first foundational pillar of a PLC. As DuFour et al. (2010a) explain:

> The mission pillar asks the question, "Why?" More specifically, it asks, "Why do we exist?" The intent of this question is to help reach agreement regarding the fundamental purpose of the school. This clarity of purpose can help establish priorities and becomes an important factor in guiding decisions. (p. 30)

We support every element of this explanation and contend that the traditional mission statement process hasn't provided consistent results. Schools should identify the fundamental purpose, then use that purpose as the lens through which to guide decisions. We know it works for some schools, but often the outcome is a product: the mission statement. We rarely see a unifying force that empowers educators to examine, clarify, and align every aspect of the school. We offer practical solutions to strengthen this important work.

According to Jeffrey Abrahams (1995), author of *The Mission Statement Book*, a mission:

- Serves as a source of direction, a kind of compass
- Engenders a sense of purposefulness, that there is a reason for working—aside from compensation
- Serves as a unifying touchstone for people and provides a sense of identity

More specifically, Abrahams (1995) defines a *mission statement* as "an enduring statement of purpose for an organization that identifies the scope of its operations and products and market terms and reflects its values and priorities" (p. 14). Would you agree that most schools do not utilize their shared mission in this manner, or in any way close to this?

Abrahams notes that a mission statement helps a company make consistent decisions, motivate employees, build organizational unity, integrate short-term objectives with long-term goals, and enhance communication. Abrahams's mission characteristics and definition could easily apply to the work of schools. But ask yourself, How many of the schools in which you've worked have applied these criteria to their shared mission?

For this definition to become reality, each staff member must become an ardent proponent of the mission and exemplify it in both words and actions—in both creed and deed. No one would deny the importance of a school rallying around its identified and agreed-on set of core principles. No one would deny the importance of every staff member's intimate awareness of identified priorities. No one would deny the importance of purposefulness and identity. Yet in almost every instance when we ask staff members to identify agreed-on ideals around which the entire school rallies, to identify a non-negotiable idea that guides the daily work of their school, to state the agreed-on purpose that serves as both compass and guide for every important decision made on campus, we almost never see agreement on what that guide is. Then, in a "Eureka!" moment, as an afterthought, the conversation turns to the school mission statement—the statement that everyone knows exists but no one can connect to the daily work of teaching, learning, and leading. We often ask our workshop participants to share their schools' mission statements from memory. What follows is often a complete loss of eye contact, uncomfortable shifting in chairs, the sudden emergency cell phone call, the impromptu bathroom break, the nervous laughter—all clear signs that people don't know.

The stated mission should permeate every aspect of school life. It should serve as your school's rallying cry and ultimate litmus test to determine what is best for improved student learning; you should not view it as an opportunity for positive public relations that eventually fades into obscurity.

The Problems With Current Approaches to Mission Statements and How to Fix Them

Many schools get caught up in creating the mission statement—the document itself—rather than creating the school described in the statement. They achieve the flawed goal of creating the document, which causes a cavalcade of related, predictable issues to surface. There are four common problems that lead schools to develop mission statements not worth the paper on which they're written. We find that schools often:

1. Share and shelve
2. Have all fluff, and no stuff
3. Engage in t-shirting
4. Accept pockets of excellence

Problem 1: Share and Shelve

Schools often invest precious time and energy discussing and developing traditional mission statements. They gather information, consider issues, answer questions, come to consensus, and decide on specific verbiage. After that, some iteration of the following steps takes place in most schools. Reflect on this sequence of steps and ask yourself if it sounds familiar.

1. We create the new mission statement.
2. We send a copy to the central office.
3. We mount the mission statement on the wall of the school foyer.
4. We post the mission statement to the school website.
5. We add the mission statement to the banner of the school newsletter.
6. We sometimes extract a catchphrase from the mission statement.
7. We go back and do what we've always done, rarely realizing that the mission statement plays no part in the daily work of teaching and learning.
8. Repeat as necessary (usually when a new leader arrives).

Problem 2: Have All Fluff, and No Stuff

Because the typical mission statement rarely serves as a guide to inform your choices, behaviors, and decisions, it is, in essence, "fluff." When you consider the time spent creating a mission statement versus the fact that its ideals seldom trickle down to the daily work of teachers and leaders, it's easy to understand the cynicism that arises. Lew Allen (2001) notes,

> [These statements are] feel-good sentiments that have been created for public relations reasons and are not serious statements of intent. Such statements as "We want our students to reach their full potential mentally, physically, and socially" or "We seek excellence in all

that we do" cry out to be ignored because they allude to ideas and results that are impossible to track. A school can never know if its students are reaching their "full potential" or if they are seeking more "excellence" this year than last. Such statements are probably meant to set a tone and to inspire people. Instead, they encourage people to ignore them. (p. 290)

As we'll explain, many schools simply ask too much of the traditional mission statement. You diminish the effectiveness of the statement when you try to make it do what it was not designed to do. Clarifying your school's mission undoubtedly has an important place in a PLC.

Problem 3: Engage in T-Shirting

Once the staff have created the mission statement, it typically works harder to develop mottos and slogans than it does to ensure that powerful practices aligned with the statement guide the work of teachers and leaders. We call this problem *t-shirting*. It means you place more emphasis on slogans for t-shirts, lanyards, coffee mugs, bumper stickers, and banners than on how your statements actually guide instructional and assessment practices and interventions. In our experience, few can articulate how their statement explicitly manifests itself in daily work. When t-shirting the new slogans and mottos without really changing daily instruction and leadership, you simply add to the confusion and ambiguity that you face, and you have nothing to show for it except some new t-shirts, lanyards, or bumper stickers.

Problem 4: Accept Pockets of Excellence

Our experience shows that schools comprise highly educated, well-intentioned, hopeful, hard-working, and dedicated staff. We want to add *committed* to that list of accolades, but we're hesitant—not because we believe that some staff aren't capable of deep commitment, but because the larger question is, *Committed to what?* Most schools lack a powerful guiding lens through which to focus that staff members understand, recognize, and repeat. Without one, schools will at best comprise hard-working people executing random acts of improvement, which result in *pockets of excellence*. These schools have no real collective commitment to engage in high-leverage, research-based best practices and risk the quality of the student learning experience because that experience will depend entirely on which teacher the student gets.

We find that many schools tolerate pockets of excellence. Why is it acceptable for one team to implement practices that you know are best for students, while you allow another team to opt out? Why resign yourself to wide variation in commitment to agreed-on best practices? While the answers to these questions may vary, they all lead back to the school's mission—defining why you exist and what school you're seeking to become, and making the collective commitment to ensure it happens.

Truth in Advertising

These four problems contribute greatly to the lack of connection between what educators say and do on a daily basis. In *Revisiting Professional Learning Communities at Work*, DuFour et al. (2008) ask the question,

> What if schools were subject to a "truth in advertising" law that required them to post their "real" mission statements—the candid statements based on actual actions and assumptions of those within the school? (p. 114)

How would your school staff respond to such a law? What would your real mission statement be? Would it be similar to one of the missions DuFour et al. (2008) suggest represent the candid missions of many American schools?

- "It is our mission to help all students learn if they are conscientious, responsible, attentive, developmentally ready, fluent in English, and come from homes with concerned parents who take an interest in their education."

- "Our mission is to create a school with an unrelenting focus on learning; failure is not an option. But ultimately, it will be the responsibility of the student and his or her parents to take advantage of the opportunities for learning."

- "Our mission is to take credit for the accomplishments of our highest-achieving students and to assign blame for low performance to others."

- "Our mission is to ensure success for all our students. We will do whatever it takes to ensure their success— provided we don't have to change the schedule, modify any of our existing practices, or adopt any new practices."

- "It is our mission to ensure the comfort and convenience of the adults in our organization. In order to promote this mission, we place a higher value on individual autonomy than we do on ensuring that all students learn. We will avoid any change or conversation that might create anxiety or discomfort or infringe on individual autonomy." (pp. 114–115)

This illustrates the simple principle that mission happens. Either the leaders and staff at your school take charge and determine your shared mission, or it will happen *to* you. If candid statements like the ones listed sound familiar to you, it's clear that you have been influenced by factors other than a collective discussion about why you exist and what you seek to become.

The Danger of Trying to Be All Things to All People

The process of clarifying your school's mission statement includes examining your school's core beliefs, fundamental purpose, assumptions, and habits. The mission statement should reflect these things. The language should be concrete, understandable, and customized specifically for your school. Ideally, your mission statement would permeate everything you do at school—embedded in your school's culture, committed to memory, modeled, and intrinsic to daily life.

The mission is not typically committed to memory, and repeating it from memory is often cumbersome at best. We propose taking one small and powerful additional step in this process: extract a non-negotiable ideal and distill it into a three- to five-word expression known as your guiding school mantra. Develop a mantra that captures the essence of your school's mission in a concise and repeatable way. Let's explore further the idea of a guiding school mantra.

Say One Thing Well: Your School's Mantra

Miguel de Cervantes defined proverbs as "short sentences drawn from long experience." Great simple ideas have the elegance and utility to function much like proverbs (Heath, 2010). This is the spirit behind mantras. A *mantra* is a statement repeated frequently to aid in concentration of thought. In Sanskrit, mantra literally means "instrument of thought." It can be a short, energy-infused statement around which your school organizes; it defines what you are and guides all internal decisions. Further, it's a powerful chant that everyone inside your school can instantly *understand, recognize,* and *repeat*—a constant reminder of what you can expect from each other. As we mentioned previously, a mantra is akin to a motto, albeit more fundamental to a school's purpose than a simple marketing slogan. It's not intended to replace your school's mission statement, but to work in concert with it.

When we think of mantras on a more global organizational scale, a very well-known company immediately comes to mind: Apple Inc. Its mantra is, "Think different." For this and other innovative companies, mantras have become a rallying point for employees and customers (Snow, 2012). Shane Snow (2012) explains the notion that mantras are *pivot proof*: "They transcend current target markets and quarterly quotas. The mantra is the guiding star, not the operating manual."

While Snow uses a corporate context, the same idea easily applies to schools. You can translate target markets and quarterly quotas into the accountability measures, test scores, or improvement initiatives you must transcend in your school. As you will see in the examples we share, a guiding school mantra should say nothing about these sorts of changes. Snow refers to a company's mantra as its guiding star. We have similarly referred to the school mantra as your North Star. A mantra is not a school improvement plan, but a lens through which you may align the school improvement plan.

Why Only Three to Five Words?

You may wonder why we strongly recommend limiting your guiding mantra to three to five words. It forces you to keep your message concise. The more succinct the mantra, the more memorable it is to stakeholders. Keep in mind that the goal is not to develop a mantra for the sake of having a short, catchy phrase that everyone knows. This is akin to motivational fluff. The mantra's catchiness simply means it's easy to keep in mind to remind one another what your school is about and to rally around for discussion and decision making.

When developing your mantra, you should be able to answer the question, What does living your guiding school mantra mean in your processes, policies, and practice? Mills (2012) contends that a mantra serves as a window into your school's story. Chip Heath and Dan Heath (2007) reinforce the short and powerful argument for the school's guiding mantra when they talk about "stickiness":

> Why do remote controls have more buttons than we ever use? The answer starts with the noble intentions of engineers. Most technology and product-design projects must combat "feature creep," the tendency for things to become incrementally more complex until they no

longer perform their original functions very well. (Kindle location 819)

We've seen that compact ideas are stickier, but that compact ideas alone aren't valuable—only ideas with profound compactness are valuable. So, to make a profound idea compact you've got to pack a lot of meaning into a little bit of messaging. (Kindle location 881)

We know exactly what you have probably been thinking: a mantra sounds like a fancy word for a slogan or a tagline. We address this next.

How Is a Mantra Different From a Slogan or Tagline?

In our work with schools, this question always surfaces. Participants want to know the differences between a guiding school mantra and a slogan. Since you are becoming a PLC, we'll draw a parallel that might resonate: the example of common formative assessments and our work with teacher teams at one school site.

While doing work with collaborative teacher teams, we noticed that one team often faced the dilemma of whether or not a particular assessment was formative or summative. A common mistake made in PLCs is thinking that a formative assessment looks distinctly different from a summative assessment. The fact is that any assessment may be either formative or summative. As Kim Bailey and Chris Jakicic (2012) note, the purpose of the assessment and how teams use the results is what really determines whether it is formative or summative, not how it's written or administered. An assessment is *formative* if the information is used to take instructional action, identify opportunities for reteaching or extension and enrichment, and inform instructional practice in time to make changes that will result in improved student learning. The same assessment can be *summative* when used to determine what students learned and to collect final grades in the unit, course, or project. In essence, formative can't be finite. The difference between a slogan and a guiding school mantra exhibits a similar parallel.

What distinguishes a mantra from a slogan is how they are used. Your guiding school mantra is a concise, repeatable, and memorable phrase that reflects your school's mission in a way that will help guide decisions, discussions, and behaviors. It's like a travel-sized version of your school's mission statement. It requires deep examination. Our goal with this stage of authentic alignment is to provide a tool that will allow schools to conveniently carry their mission and keep it front, center, and on display in every aspect of school life.

Creating Your Guiding School Mantra: The Tip of the Iceberg

You may look at this next section and wonder why there are several steps in the process of developing your school's mantra. How many stages can it possibly take to come up with potential mantras such as the following?

- Every child, every day
- In this, we believe
- Whatever it takes
- Doing our best, every day
- Learning for all

One of the most common pitfalls in PLC implementation is the temptation to take shortcuts in the process. If the aim were simply to develop a three- to five-word phrase, then we would call it a slogan. Your guiding school mantra may look like a simple catchphrase or slogan to others, but to every person in your organization, it will be only the tip of the iceberg. You know that this idiom typically means that there is a large problem looming undetected beyond what looks like a small problem. And you know the meaning behind it, that icebergs reveal only a small portion above the surface of the water. The much larger body of the iceberg remains beneath the surface, out of sight. However, we're using this idiom in a more positive way. Instead of a problem, we see the larger body of the iceberg supporting the visible tip—your guiding school mantra—as shown in figure 3.1.

As with every stage of authentic alignment, don't look at developing a mantra as simply a task to complete; the benefit is in the process—the dialogue.

There is an old adage reminding that before you can know where you're going, you have to take stock of where you've been. Early in Ken's first principalship, he made the mistake of dismissing this adage while working to build a culture of collective responsibility. With wide-eyed enthusiasm, the optimism of ten men, the energy of twenty men, and an ambitious vision, Ken, with great skill, proceeded to alienate his entire staff within the first week of taking the job. Ken knew that this reaction wasn't a result of any lack of people skills or caring on his part. It was based on two major errors in leadership: (1) although he had a phenomenal vision, it wasn't a shared vision, and (2) he looked to the future without acknowledging the past. For better or worse, the school's history is important to consider in the context of building a culture of collective responsibility. Fortunately for Ken, this realization dawned quickly, and in time to salvage the process. Ken first had to show a level of transparency by admitting the error of his ways. While this was not his intention, it built trust between him and the staff. They collectively took a step back and learned about the rich history of their school. As soon as the exploration of their history began, Ken knew it would inform their mission and their mantra.

School History Map Activity: Where Your School Has Been

This powerful activity invites team members to tell stories about their school and the people associated with it. Learning and exploring your school's history creates context, deepens shared knowledge, and can shed light on the dimensions of the existing culture. It is

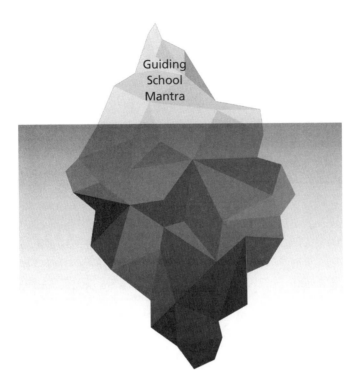

Figure 3.1: The guiding school mantra—The tip of the iceberg.

very useful for new staff members to hear a wealth of stories. Then they see how they fit into the school's history. You can even invite retired and former staff members to share memories.

Step One

Using a roll of butcher paper, shelf paper, or the back of an old roll of wallpaper, make a timeline of the decades since the school opened, leaving ample space between decades (or years) for stories. Be sure to include space for recent stories as well.

Mark the paper with a variety of prompts to help staff recall their stories, such as:

- Events that took place
- Key people or groups

- Physical changes to the building
- Educational policy changes

Attach the paper to the wall. Provide artifacts like old yearbooks, photo albums, and newspaper clippings to help jog memories. You'll also need colored pens and sticky notes.

Step Two

Divide the staff into random groups or by the era in which they began working at the school. Tell them that their task is to write down on the sticky notes provided any stories that they can recall and the year (or decade) in which the event occurred. Then they place a sticky note on the butcher paper in the appropriate area. Here are some additional prompts that might help activate people's memories.

- A time you were most proud of the school
- A time you were most sorry
- Historic events that shaped the school
- A memorable student
- The class from hell
- Your worst or best lesson
- A random act of kindness
- Reunions and graduations
- Clothing, music, and hairstyles that were popular
- Traditions like annual school trips or events

Staff members write down their stories and attach them securely to the chart.

Step Three

In this step, participants "walk the wall" reflecting on the items on the chart. Armed with the template shown in figure 3.2, participants should begin processing the events their colleagues have identified as important to their shared history. This processing helps learners make connections between their school's history, their own educational experiences, and eventually helps inform priorities and next steps.

What Happened?	Why Was It Important?	How Can the Group Use This Information?	Notes

Figure 3.2: School history map activity processing template.

*Visit **go.solution-tree.com/plcbooks** for a reproducible version of this figure.*

Step Four

The debriefing of this activity is very important. Ask participants for their reflections about the lessons learned and the overall themes, patterns, or trends. Invite comments, especially from newcomers. Be prepared for emotional stories, too. What predictions and recommendations do staff members have for what the future holds?

The stories told in front of the group are an important first step in mission building. As Alan Wilken says (quoted in Peters & Austin, 1985), stories can affect performance. They can be powerful ways to motivate, teach, and spread enthusiasm, loyalty, and commitment. They can also serve the equally powerful purpose of perpetuating cynicism, distrust, and disbelief. They reveal underlying beliefs or doubts people feel but are unwilling to confess directly. While Wilken speaks in a broad organizational context, we have often seen what he describes play out in schools. This activity is a first step in both assessing and building culture. The insights you glean from the school history map activity help you assess your current reality and place school culture in a very human context.

Assessing Your Current Reality: Where Your School Is Now

The very core of a PLC is a focus on and a commitment to the learning of each student. The PLC process asks that you move from a generic mission statement to a culture that centers learning in its day-to-day work. This requires that you explore:

- Where you are
- Where you've been
- Where you're going

One of the ways to do this is to complete the A Data Picture of Our School assessment DuFour et al. (2010a) provide in *Learning by Doing* (2nd edition, pages 24–26, also available on the All Things PLC website [www.allthingsplc.info/tools-resources]). The self-assessment asks for data that are concrete and factual. The data picture will help you and your staff see the difference between your intended reality and your actual reality.

Using the information collected in the previous step, reflect on these guiding questions. Note that some questions require individual reflection before any public sharing.

1. What do you think is the most basic, fundamental purpose of your school? If you can sum up in one declaration what your school stands for, what would it be? What evidence can you point to that supports your answer?

2. What are the data telling you? How has your school gone beyond writing a mission statement to embed learning in

the culture of your school as its core purpose? What evidence can you point to that supports your answer?

3. Reflect on this statement: "When something is truly a priority in an organization, people do not hope it happens; they develop and implement specific plans to ensure that it happens" (DuFour, DuFour, Eaker, & Many, 2010b, p. 8). What gets planned for in your school?

4. It has been said that what gets monitored, gets done. Describe how priorities are monitored in your school and how results are shared with the staff.

5. Do you think it's important to help all students learn or just give them the chance to learn? What about your school?

6. Organizations demonstrate priorities through the allocation of resources—time, money, and human resources. Are the resources in your school allocated according to proclaimed priorities?

7. What percentage of unsuccessful students is acceptable to your school?

Your staff can reflect on these questions in small groups and as a whole team. In addition to these important reflections, teams should share other data when building shared knowledge about the current reality, such as evidence of student learning, disaggregated data about how different subgroups achieve, disciplinary data, transition or graduation rates, and parent or community surveys. This helps paint an accurate picture of the school's current reality.

Define Your Desired Reality: Where Your School Is Going

Next, explore the following questions in small groups:

1. Now that you have a better sense of your school's reality, what *should* matter most and take precedence in your school?

2. What would you identify as the three most important priorities that you need to address in the service of *learning for all* by your school?

3. What would you now identify as the *most important* priority of your school?

4. What do you now believe is the most basic, fundamental purpose of your school? What behaviors should you observe that support your answer?

5. Are you willing to embrace the core purpose of learning for all? Just as important, are you also willing to live by the two fundamental assumptions associated with learning for all?

   • We believe that all students can learn at high levels.

   • We take collective responsibility to ensure they learn.

6. What are some of the behaviors you should see if you are focused on your core purpose?

7. Are you willing to accept what *collective commitment* means? This involves committing to agreed-on best practices. (We will explore those practices in the Now in chapter 6, page 125.)

Characteristics of a Guiding School Mantra

A good guiding school mantra is simple, memorable, positive, grounded, and uniquely yours. Let's briefly explore each of these elements.

1. **Simple:** Your guiding school mantra should convey one simple idea in as few words as possible. You can't mean everything to everybody, so just focus on one specific thing and say it well.

2. **Memorable:** It is vital that your guiding school mantra finds its way into your staff's subconscious, to make sure they remember it and can repeat it.

3. **Positive:** Your guiding school mantra should encourage an optimistic outlook for your staff.

4. **Grounded:** Your mantra must be grounded in the two conditions necessary for collective responsibility in a PLC.

   • We believe that all students can learn at high levels.

   • We make the collective commitment to ensure learning occurs for every student.

5. **Uniquely yours:** Make sure your guiding school mantra is uniquely about your school. As a staff, you should feel ownership and investment.

Now that you have explored the bulk of the iceberg in the previous step, generate ideas for your school's guiding mantra.

Provide a Compelling Context

When you ask staff members to offer potential guiding school mantras for consideration, you want them to connect to the exercise on an emotional level. In our work with educators, we address groups developing mantras in the following way. Think about your sons or daughters rather than the students in your school. If you're not a parent, think of a child so special in your life that you'd offer your life for his or hers. With that in mind, imagine that you've been charged with suggesting the guiding mantra for their school. What three- to five-word phrase captures the essence of your beliefs and commitments and fulfills the five criteria for mantras—simple, memorable, positive, grounded, and uniquely yours?

Develop a Personal I-Message Commitment

At the surface level, the guiding school mantra gives you a concise, energy-infused idea around which to rally your school. But you can take its power a step beyond inspiration and motivation; it also enables every person on staff to declare a personal commitment to live the guiding school mantra in the context of his or her specific role at the school. Once staff members draft their suggestions, the next step is for each person to declare a personal commitment to live with their guiding school mantra. This is done by developing a personal I-message. The term *I-message* has been used in various types of conflict resolution protocols for decades (Gordon & Edwards, 1995). Let's look at an example: The agreed-on guiding school mantra of Northside Elementary is "Every child is my child." An I-message for this mantra might include, *I will to act on behalf of all students—not just my students.*

Hold a Small-Group Share

Next, share the proposed mantras and I-messages. Allow each team-mate to briefly explain his or her mantra, its meaning, and his or her inspiration. Ask groups to narrow it down to the top mantra per group using the fist-to-five process for consensus outlined by DuFour et al. (2008; see figure 3.3). Examples of school guiding mantras and personal I-messages appear in table 3.1.

Another option is to share the guiding mantra ideas on chart paper and post them on the wall. Take a break and conduct a gallery walk around the room. Look at the mantras and eliminate those that duplicate or overlap. You can also use technology to provide anonymity if that is a concern at your school. Software applications such as Poll Everywhere (www.polleverywhere.com) allow for anonymous real-time voting. You can create an option to submit mantras (for example, "In three to five words, what would you suggest for your school's guiding mantra?"), and then to provide an I-message, and later on, for team members to vote. Although not as desirable as team collaboration, this may be a more practical option depending on your situation.

Fist-to-Five Process

The facilitator then asks every member of the group to indicate how he or she feels about that direction based on a scale of fist to five.

Fist: "That is not a good idea, and I am going to block you if you try to implement it."

(In other words, a *no* vote.)

One finger: "I do not agree, but I promise not to block it."

Two fingers: "I do not agree, but I will work for it."

Three fingers: "I am neutral."

> **Four fingers:** "It is a good idea, and I will work for it."
>
> **Five fingers:** "It is a great idea, and I will be one of the leaders in implementing it."
>
> Once every member in the group has indicated how he or she feels, the facilitator should turn to any blocker and ask, "To what part of our current proposal do you object?" The reason for doing this is twofold. One reason for having input into decision making is that often one individual can see a particular problem with the current decision that the rest of the group has not seen. If the person holds up a fist, it is possible for the rest of the group to understand the objection and compromise. Second, input is helpful because it places the responsibility or accountability where it rightfully belongs: with the person who has an objection. This forces that person to state openly to the rest of his or her colleagues exactly what he or she objects to and why. This reduces the possibility that the individual will object simply because he or she doesn't feel well that day or because he or she does not like the person who proposed the idea.

Source: DuFour et al., 2008, page 138.

Figure 3.3: Fist-to-five process.

Table 3.1: Examples of Mantras and I-Messages

Mantras	I-Messages
We work as a village.	I commit to embrace a true collaborative culture. I will pull my weight as part of my interdependent team.
We believe you can achieve!	I embrace accountability for our results, and I am constantly asking, "Is there something else I can do?"

Continued on next page →

| Every child is my child. | I consider every child my child, and the failure of any one of them is not an option. I am humble enough to ask for help, and think abundantly enough to share resources and best practices. |
| Tomorrow depends on today. | I will spend time focusing on factors I can control, and hold my teammates accountable to do the same. |

Finding Your Center

Your mission should be at the center of everything you do; defining your shared mission is a critical step in the transformation from a traditional school into a PLC. This step in the authentic alignment process helps you connect with your mission by taking you step by step through a powerful examination of your existing school culture and helping you identify the essence of your mission by creating a guiding school mantra. Congratulations! You have assessed your current reality, confronted some brutal facts, identified your fundamental purpose, and identified a mantra around which to rally. Now you are ready to apply what you've learned to give deeper meaning to your daily work, align your efforts, and invest and engage in your collective responsibility in a PLC.

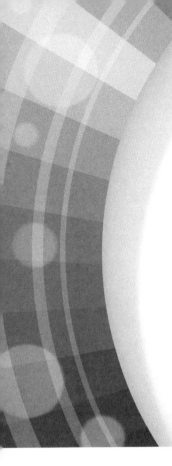

Chapter 4

Envisioning: The Eye

Take up one idea. Make that one idea your life—think of it, dream of it, live on that idea. Let the brain, muscles, nerves, every part of your body, be full of that idea, and just leave every other idea alone. This is the way to success.

—SWAMI VIVEKANANDA

Envisioning, the Eye, is a process to help you develop a clear, compelling, shared vision of the school you seek to become. This step in authentic alignment helps to strengthen the second foundational pillar of a PLC: vision. *Merriam-Webster* defines *vision* as "something that you imagine: a picture that you see in your mind" and "something that you see or dream" (Vision, n.d.). We love the *Merriam-Webster* definition because your school's vision should stretch you. Timothy D. Kanold (2011) supports the notion of stretching when he assures us that "the concept of *vision* often feels vague and out of reach. Yet vision is and always will be one of the most potent change weapons in your leadership life" (p. 11).

The vision pillar asks, "What must we become in order to accomplish our fundamental purpose?" In pursuing this question, you and your staff attempt to create a compelling, attractive, realistic future:

a high-definition description of your ideal school, the school you seek to become. Researchers in and outside of education routinely note the importance of developing shared vision. Pam Robbins and Harvey Alvy (2004) state that a vision "serves as a compass, lending direction to organizational members' behavior" (p. 3). The Great Schools Partnership (2014) defines shared vision as "a public declaration that schools . . . use to describe their high-level goals for the future—what they hope to achieve if they successfully fulfill their organizational purpose or mission."

Starting a movement begins with standing for something. Standing for something is critical to a movement, but it's not enough. Vision is the ideal picture of your school's movement. Vision helps us define what our ideal school looks like, practically and literally.

What You Focus on Grows

Vision, when directed well, becomes the driver of change. Your vision describes your school's loftiest ideals, reflects your fundamental purpose as an organization, and chronicles your hopes for your students' capabilities after graduating. In the world of education, the creation of a vision is nothing new. Your vision should be a descriptive statement of what your school will be like at a specified time in the future. It uses descriptive words or phrases and sometimes pictures to illustrate what one would expect to see, hear, and experience in the school at that time. It engages all stakeholders in answering such questions as:

- Who are we serving?
- What school do we seek to become?
- What do we want for our students when they leave our care?
- What does a day in the life look like at our ideal school?
- What ideal school would we want for our own students?
- What are our aspirations for the school?
- Why will there be a waiting list to attend our school?

Our experiences in schools across North America reveal that too few schools and districts engage in the exploration of these types of questions. Think about movements that have changed the course of human history. When you study them, you find that they involved action in the present, driven by a challenging, compelling, and worthwhile future ideal. Some movements have had such a compelling vision that people have been willing to give their lives for the cause. While our work in schools isn't associated with that immediate threat, it is noble and definitely has life-altering ripple effects. The authentic alignment process helps you to challenge your existing paradigms to clarify and align or realign with your vision.

Shared vision involves seeing past your current circumstances. Whether your school is elevating itself from a history of low achievement or facing a good-to-great scenario by meeting expectations and wanting to move toward further success, the Eye is a powerful step. Kanold (2011) refers to this process of envisioning as the "discipline of vision and values" and calls it "the leadership work of developing and delivering a compelling picture of the school's future that produces energy, passion, and action in yourself and others." He goes on to say that this work ensures that "the vision guides the decision-making actions for your district, school, or program area" and that it is "one of your most potent leadership tools for the development of coherent and sustainable actions" (Kanold, 2011, pp. 6–7).

Research points to the importance of creating a shared vision and shows that consistency in teacher practice has a positive impact on the outcomes for all students. David Reynolds and Charles Teddlie (2000) point out:

> The generation of a learning community amongst staff in which all members share good practice, act as critical friends, and engage in a process of mutual education and re-education is clearly essential in the continuation of a positive school culture over time, as well as in its creation. (p. 148)

Your school's vision as examined in the Eye stage is not only a catalyst for action and decision making, it's also an expression of optimism. Can you imagine a leader enlisting others in a cause by saying, "I'd like you to join me in doing the ordinary better" (Kouzes & Posner, 1987, p. 133)? Of course not! Your school's vision should challenge you at the same time it describes your destination. Mike Muir (2012) uses the following metaphor to illustrate the importance of a shared vision for your school: What if you were a sailboat captain? Let's even say you've got a great boat and a wonderful crew. Together you've done a lot of sailing. Maybe you even work well together and know how to collaboratively operate the boat to maneuver well and go really fast, coaxing forth its peak performance. But what does all this mean if you have no destination? Or worse, what would happen if each crew member had a different picture of where you were headed? What would the outcome be then? In fact, you may only be able to judge your success when you measure it against your progress to a specific destination.

As you work through the following activities and reflections to help strengthen your vision, be cautious when using the terms *mission statement* and *vision statement*. These are often used interchangeably. While some educators and schools may loosely define the two terms, or even blur the traditional lines that have separated them, there appears to be general agreement in the education community on the major distinctions between a mission and a vision. A vision statement expresses a hoped-for future reality, while a mission statement declares the practical commitments and actions that a school believes are needed to achieve its vision. While a vision statement describes the end goal—the change sought by a school—a mission statement may describe its broad academic and operational assurances, as well as its commitment to its students and community (Great Schools Partnership, 2014). What they have in common is that they serve as a guide for connecting your decisions and your described destination.

The Untapped Potential of Visioning

Before we delve into the specifics on how envisioning (the Eye) supports PLCs, let's take a step back and explore the powerful creative properties of vision. We often ask school staff members about their knowledge of shared vision. When we ask what the vision statement is, hands don't fly into the air from sheer enthusiasm. The typical answers we receive are ones like:

- It's an extension of the mission statement.
- It's what we want to see in the future.
- It's what we hope to become as a school.
- It's the statement of what we hope our students achieve.

Some of these answers aren't far off the mark. A shared vision statement is not simply an extension of your school's mission statement, but it definitely does help to paint a picture of what we seek to become, what we will do for our school, and an ideal picture of what we want for our students when they leave our care.

After asking what shared vision is, we then ask educators, Why is it important, and what impact does it have on your daily work? In response to this question, we often face silence, so we try another question regarding intent: why do schools engage in the work of developing a shared vision? More often than not, the responses to this question reflect the feeling that the activity is being done due to mindless precedent. In other words, we are developing the vision for our school because that's what you do after you complete the mission statement. Another popular response is that it's what every school does.

This is what we call a "shake me awake" moment. Suspend what you believe you know about the power of vision and consider looking outside of education to see how the process is leveraged. We offer some relatable parallels from sports and our personal lives.

World-class athletes rely on visioning as an essential part of their practice and preparation. Before competition on the court, the ice, the course, and so on, athletes see themselves playing the entire game or moving through their performance in their mind's eye. They intentionally make time in their day, quiet their mind, and picture the event taking place. This includes every shot, bounce, putt, and so on. They visualize powerful game-changing moments, challenges, turning points, and victory. Much like we help schools do, they paint an ideal picture of what they want to achieve. They understand that what they focus on grows. For example, Professional Golfers' Association legend Jack Nicklaus credits much of his success to how often and how vividly he would play all eighteen holes of a golf tournament mentally. He would focus on every shot, every chip, every putt, as well as the flight of the ball on every shot. By the time he got to the course for the first round of the tournament, playing often felt like the review of what he'd already done. This process helped him to be successful in his career. National Hockey League legend Wayne Gretzky took the same approach to his hockey career. He would visualize every shot, every assist, the flight and rotation of the puck. This focused mental practice contributed positively to both his practice and skill in game play. National Basketball Association legend Michael Jordan not only employed the same strategies and practices of visualization, he also had that level of focus on the practice court. Jordan not only held himself to the high standards he envisioned, but he also expected the very best of his teammates during every minute of every practice. This focus made many of his most amazing career moments seem routine, because he had played the moments over and over again in his mind.

Visualization has become an integral tool in the area of peak performance in general. We use three well-known athletes as examples; however, visualization as a component of peak performance is not limited to high-performing athletes. It's common in many fields inside and outside of sports. Managers, coaches, and others are making it a priority to engage those with whom they work in protocols that allow them to see past their current circumstances and get clear on their ideal future.

Visioning doesn't have to be professional—it can be personal as well. In our work in education, we ask staff members to consider the importance of visioning as it relates to their work in getting their teaching degrees. As students, we all had to overcome obstacles and complete difficult tasks. Consider the courses you took, the assignments you completed, the essays and research papers you wrote, the study sessions, the all-nighters, the computer problems, every can of Red Bull (or if you're from our generation, perhaps every can of Mountain Dew).

You're probably recalling stories of tragedy and triumph, pleasure and pain. You did all of these things with an end result in mind: earning your degree. Imagine doing all that work without the end in mind. Would you volunteer to engage in all those things if the road didn't end with a college degree? Who would opt for such stress and financial investment if there were no compelling end goal? Our point in using this example is this: one of the reasons you endured all the challenges and adversity, the highs and lows of earning a degree, is because the end goal was compelling enough for you to invest the energy and focus to do so. For however long it took you to earn your degree, you kept your eye on your vision and the purpose behind the vision—whether to fulfill a dream of working with kids, make a difference in communities, increase your income, achieve employment mobility, or make your parents proud—the bottom line is your reason for completing your degree was inspiring enough for you to aspire to take the next steps.

The exact same principle applies to your work in schools. You have to come together around a shared purpose of your ideal school to create a vision to guide and inform everything you do. It will provide fuel in the best of times and the fortitude to endure during the challenging times. Developing your shared vision allows you to overcome challenges, problem solve effectively, and deal with adversity.

The Three Levels of Envisioning

Now that you have a more thorough understanding of the potential of visioning, your next challenge is to revisit your school's or district's shared vision and make sure it has become an integral part of your school's culture. In an effort to support the vision pillar of the PLC foundation, we have developed three levels of exploring your school's shared vision. Each of these levels builds on the others. The three levels are:

- Level I—Inspiration
- Level II—Aspiration
- Level III—Perspiration

Let's examine each of these three levels.

Level I—Inspiration

Inspiring visions rally people to a greater purpose, even if they seem daunting at first. Although it seems counterintuitive, the best way to lead people into the future is to connect with them deeply in the present (Kouzes & Posner, 2009). The only visions that stick are shared visions that develop from listening very closely to others, appreciating their hopes, and attending to their needs: "The best leaders are able to bring their people into the future because they engage in the oldest form of research: They observe the human condition" (Kouzes & Posner, 2009, pp. 20–21). It doesn't matter if your school has a vision if you don't know it, have a connection to it, or are incapable of articulating it. Your school's vision can be specific, concise, and consistent, but if it fails to touch staff on an emotional level, it will fail and be doomed to a life of hanging on a wall or on your website banner. Your school's shared vision has to be large enough for every person to see his or her personal vision within it. Not only does your shared vision have to speak to ideal conditions your school seeks to achieve, but the people who are making it happen must also see themselves getting better in the process. Is your school's shared vision inspiring? Does it energize you? Is the future it describes so compelling that it spurs you to grow more, to learn more, to be more, to get uncomfortable, and to be your best?

We have to do more than guilt educators into being their best. When we understand what motivates people, an inspiring shared vision can be a galvanizing force that is clear and universally understood by all stakeholders. When we work with schools on the process of reculturing from the inside out, the single most commonly expressed concern is buy-in from staff. "Selling" an idea has less impact than helping staff invest in an idea of an inspiring picture of their ideal future. If, after honest reflection, you conclude that your shared vision lacks the element of inspiration, then you and your staff would benefit from taking a step back and engaging in the activities in each of the three envisioning levels. They're designed to activate your thinking in ways that begin to provide a picture of your future desired state.

Consider the following questions to reflect on your school's vision and recapture your inspiration.

1. What is your school's shared vision?

2. In one sentence, write what you would like school to provide to your child, a question our friend and colleague Mike Mattos often asks in his work in schools.

3. What is the image we have of our school in our own minds? In our district? In our community? Are these images we want to represent our school?

4. Does our school's vision mesh with our answers to the two previous questions?

The inspiration level is important to shared vision, but one of the major reasons visioning is so underutilized in school cultures is because schools rarely move past the inspiration level of vision. Schools often *start* and *stop* at being inspired and find themselves back in a rut with their efforts needing to be reenergized. Over time, the work of shared vision can resemble the aftermath of a motivational talk: after the initial hoopla is over, the vision loses its potency and collective efforts suffer from a lack of focus. The ideals you have identified in the inspiration level alone are not enough to bring success.

Level II—Aspiration

Once you have rekindled the kind of shared understanding that makes your staff collectively wide-eyed and wired to take action, you move into level II, aspiration. The aspiration level asks the question, What does the school we seek to create look like? (Keep in mind, this is not the point where we gather collective commitments to agreed-on best practices. Collective commitments around best practices come later once we have full and clear understanding of exactly what is required to create our ideal school.) At this next level, we are simply unpacking aligned practices and then eventually committing to building shared knowledge around each of those practices.

First, reflect on the following questions:

1. Envision yourself five years in the future. You just opened the newspaper and are reading about your school. What does the headline say?

2. What are five specific commitments your staff made that could have contributed to the headline and the accompanying story?

In the Why stage, you learned that PLCs have at their core "learning for all" as a fundamental purpose. With that in mind, you have almost forty years of practical evidence to draw from that supports best practices in a PLC. When you take collective responsibility for ensuring high levels of learning for all students, your school does the following:

- Commits to a collaborative culture, rather than having teachers work in isolation

- Identifies the most essential targets every student must master at every grade level and in every course

- Constantly measures effectiveness and improves instruction through the use of teacher-created common formative assessments

- Systematically responds, by name and by need, to any student experiencing difficulty learning or who has already mastered the content

At the aspiration level, the goal is to identify or reconnect with this essential work required to aspire to our ideal school. Reflection regarding these best practices should reveal areas where your school or district is strong, as well as opportunities for learning, growth, and improvement.

- When you commit to a collaborative culture, rather than having teachers work in isolation, what does this look like?

- What does it look like to identify the most essential targets every student must master at every grade level and in every course?

- What does it look like when teams constantly measure their effectiveness?

- What does it look like when teams systematically respond when students experience difficulty and when students already know the content?

Reflecting on these commitments helps your teams develop a vision of what they aspire to create and build shared knowledge of what is needed to get there. The final stage of envisioning, perspiration, takes these commitments to build shared knowledge and helps teams identify their strengths and weaknesses.

Level III—Perspiration

The third level is aptly named *perspiration*. The purpose of the stage is for your staff to evaluate areas in which members must build shared knowledge. Committing to and investing in a shared vision of your school's ideal future is much more than capturing a chorus of yeses at the peak of emotional motivation. For anyone to truly invest in what it takes to achieve your compelling vision, you have to build knowledge of what it takes to achieve the vision. Collective commitment takes root when staff members have absolute clarity on shared and expected best practices and on specific observable behaviors and protocols embedded in each of those practices. The perspiration level is the opportunity for staff to assess strengths and opportunities, learn together, and move ahead as a PLC.

As a team, look at each of the critical issues in figure 4.1 and do the following:

1. Determine the level of implementation of each issue by selecting the appropriate designation:

    a. Fully implemented and in place (IP)

    b. Not fully implemented and working on it (WO)

    c. Not yet implemented and not yet being addressed (NY)

    Note that any item determined as being in place must be supported by product evidence.

2. Determine whether each issue is a curriculum issue (C), an assessment issue (A), or a team issue (T). Note that some issues can be more than one of these designations. For the purpose of the data analysis later in this activity, agree on one designation. It's much more important that the team agree on the implementation level.

3. Indicate the implementation level and type of issue in the space before each item (for example, IP/C).

____ 1.	We have organized staff members into meaningful collaborative teams that support each member's daily responsibilities.
____ 2.	We provide protected time for collaborative teams to meet on a weekly basis (if possible).
____ 3.	We have identified team norms and protocols to guide us in working together.

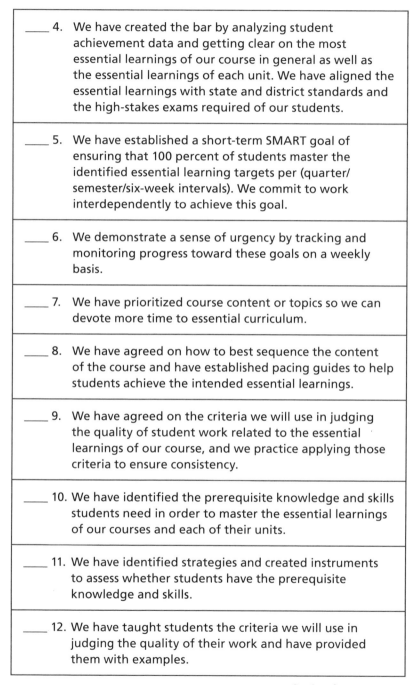

_____ 4. We have created the bar by analyzing student achievement data and getting clear on the most essential learnings of our course in general as well as the essential learnings of each unit. We have aligned the essential learnings with state and district standards and the high-stakes exams required of our students.

_____ 5. We have established a short-term SMART goal of ensuring that 100 percent of students master the identified essential learning targets per (quarter/semester/six-week intervals). We commit to work interdependently to achieve this goal.

_____ 6. We demonstrate a sense of urgency by tracking and monitoring progress toward these goals on a weekly basis.

_____ 7. We have prioritized course content or topics so we can devote more time to essential curriculum.

_____ 8. We have agreed on how to best sequence the content of the course and have established pacing guides to help students achieve the intended essential learnings.

_____ 9. We have agreed on the criteria we will use in judging the quality of student work related to the essential learnings of our course, and we practice applying those criteria to ensure consistency.

_____ 10. We have identified the prerequisite knowledge and skills students need in order to master the essential learnings of our courses and each of their units.

_____ 11. We have identified strategies and created instruments to assess whether students have the prerequisite knowledge and skills.

_____ 12. We have taught students the criteria we will use in judging the quality of their work and have provided them with examples.

Continued on next page →

Figure 4.1: Critical issues assessment chart.

_____ 13. We have developed frequent common formative assessments that help us to determine each student's mastery of essential learnings.

_____ 14. We have established the proficiency standard we want each student to achieve on each skill and concept examined with our common formative assessments.

_____ 15. We use the results of our common formative assessments to assist each other in building on strengths and addressing weaknesses as part of a process of continuous improvement designed to help students at higher levels.

_____ 16. We use the results of our common formative assessments to identify students who need additional time and support to master essential learning, and we work within the systems and processes of the school to ensure they receive that support.

_____ 17. We have developed common summative assessments that help us assess the strengths and weaknesses of our program.

_____ 18. We have established the proficiency standard we want each student to achieve on each skill and concept examined with our common summative assessments.

*Visit **go.solution-tree.com/plcbooks** for a reproducible version of this figure.*

Next, as a team, place the number of each issue on the grid in figure 4.2 (developed by Virginia Mahlke). Determine the appropriate cell for each issue based on how you assessed it in figure 4.1. See the sample (also courtesy of Virginia Mahlke) in figure 4.3.

Next, use the following questions to guide your discussion and analysis of the data:

1. Which cell contained the most tallies?

2. In which areas do we have the strongest implementation?

	C	A	T
IP			
WO			
NY			

Source: Virginia Mahlke.

Figure 4.2: Critical issues summary template.

*Visit **go.solution-tree.com/plcbooks** for a reproducible version of this figure.*

	C	A	T
IP	11, 12, 18	17	1, 7
WO	10	2, 3, 16	4, 15
NY	6	5, 8, 9, 13	14

Source: Virginia Mahlke.

Figure 4.3: Sample critical issues summary template.

*Visit **go.solution-tree.com/plcbooks** for a reproducible version of this figure.*

3. Do we have primarily curriculum issues, assessment issues, or team issues?

4. Where are our challenges and opportunities to build shared knowledge?

5. In what order should we build shared knowledge to have the greatest impact on student achievement?

6. What action plans and next steps will we create to move forward based on these data?

Bringing Shared Vision to Life

Can you begin to see the importance of bringing shared vision to life? Inspiration in isolation is never enough. Inspiration without next steps is nothing but motivational fluff and results in dismissal of the vision over time. At the same time, identifying best practices in isolation is never enough. You can provide a plethora of research, evidence, and data supporting specific best practices, but if there is nothing to which people can aspire, you will get compliance at best, resentment at worst. For many schools, this is the condition that exists within their walls.

By envisioning what you want your school to become, you develop a sense of direction for growth. This clarity builds momentum. It allows team members to recognize incremental breakthroughs that lead to significant growth. Kouzes and Posner (1987) liken the power of clarity to driving a car:

> Clarity of vision [is important], *especially* when you're going fast. How fast can you drive in the fog without risking your own or other people's lives? How comfortable are you riding in a car with someone else who drives that fast in the fog? Are you able to go faster when it's foggy or when it's clear? We're better able to anticipate the switchbacks and bumps in the road when we can see ahead. There are always going to be times when the sun hides behind the clouds or fog makes it difficult to maneuver, but when it comes to traveling at Internet speed it's definitely preferable to be able to see farther ahead. (pp. 114, 125)

Timothy D. Kanold (2011) reminds us that once it's established, the vision becomes the voice of authority for our work and actions. A PLC leader commits to the adage, "A shared followership is built not on whom to follow, but on what to follow" (p. 27). There is often a huge difference between the school you desire and your willingness to behave in ways essential to creating such a school. Seeing the school you want is the first step in the journey to making the vision become reality. If the vision is truly shared, it will be evident in both the climate (how a school feels) and the culture (how business is done) of the school (Robbins & Alvy, 2004). In the next chapter, we explore how to link the Eye with your daily work by connecting, or the How.

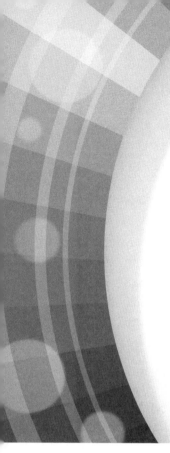

Chapter 5

Connecting: The How

Whether you create it or you condone it, you own it.

—TOM HIERCK

The third stage of authentic alignment helps strengthen the third pillar of a PLC: values. By turning your work from words to an actual force to propel learning forward, you start a powerful movement of staff members aligning around collective commitments that result in positive change. By the time you begin connecting with the How, you have already strengthened your shared mission by developing a guiding school mantra (the Why) and clarified your vision for your school (the Eye). This is an important juncture in the process of moving from compliance to commitment and represents a tipping point in the evolution of mission and vision statements from words only to embedded behaviors. They must go from something you check off a list to something you use to drive all of your decisions. As Simon Sinek (2009) states, "A why without the how, passion without structure, has a very high probability of failure" (p. 184).

In the How stage, schools strengthen the next foundational step in the essential work of a PLC:

1. Creating a collaborative culture
2. Clearly defining what every student needs to learn
3. Constantly measuring effectiveness
4. Systematically responding when students do and do not learn

We have seen schools in which the staff are in agreement about their shared mission and vision but left to their own discretion to decide what it looks like in action—what people actually do. This discretion can lead to ineffective practices and teacher isolation—what we described earlier as random acts of improvement. Teachers expend energy on a myriad of strategies and practices, and dilute their potential for maximum impact.

In *Revisiting Professional Learning Communities at Work*, DuFour et al. (2008) profile the work of Janel Keating, the superintendent of the White River School District in Buckley, Washington. Ken has had the honor of working closely with Janel, who is now a colleague, by providing professional development in her district. On the first day back to school for staff, and before turning the staff over to Ken for staff development, Janel challenged the group with two questions that generated such clarity that they inspired this stage of the authentic alignment process. She asked, "What would it look like if we really meant what we say about all students learning at high levels?" and "What would people see us doing?" These two questions set the context for PLC work clearly and simply, yet powerfully. This is what the How is about.

Janel learned from experience that instead of leaving best practices to the discretion of every individual staff member, she needed to lead staff in an exploration of a few high-leverage best practices that:

• Reflected their shared mission
• Aligned with their compelling shared vision
• Communicated the belief that every student could learn at high levels

- Demonstrated their ownership to ensure learning for every student
- Promoted learning for all
- Improved student learning and teacher learning

If we were to create a column on a sheet of paper for each of these six bulleted items, we could fill the page with practices and initiatives we deem high leverage. However, in a PLC, we narrow down practices and initiatives to what we call the essential work: the agreed-on behavioral commitments for staff members. As DuFour et al. (2008) state, "The mission of a school or district is not revealed by what people say, but rather, by what they do" (p. 114).

This work is not *optional* or *suggested*—it is *essential*. You can deem something important without it being necessary for success. But when something is judged essential, it is vital to success. And so it is with the essential work of a PLC. It is vital, non-negotiable, and in no way optional. Therefore:

- Creating a collaborative culture is essential to PLC success
- Clearly defining what every student needs to learn is essential to PLC success
- Constantly measuring our effectiveness is essential to PLC success
- Systematically responding when students do and do not learn is essential to PLC success

We will explore each of these essential PLC elements and provide reflection questions to help guide your work in connecting the How. Janel Keating helped move educators in her district from rhetoric to action when she pressed her staff to answer the questions, "What would it look like in our schools if we really meant it when we said our fundamental purpose is to ensure all students learn? What would people see us doing?", and it helped her district soar rather than stall in its PLC transformation.

A secondary focus in the How is to explore and reinforce some of the common characteristics of schools where PLCs flourish and schools where they stall. We have seen many schools in which the staff believe they're implementing the PLC process effectively. In reality, we instead find patterns, habits, and actions that fall short of the commitment required for PLCs to be embedded into the culture.

In this step, we describe three levels of commitment to the work of your PLC.

1. Is your school *flirting* with PLCs? We will identify statements, practices, and habits common among schools flirting with the PLC process. By *flirting*, we mean surface exploration or implementation. This is the stage in which staff members make excuses, do not always comply, implement poorly, do not connect with the moral imperative, and do not align with the shared mission or vision. The flirting stage is when schools claim to implement PLCs, but wonder more about the PLC process, implement out of compliance, or do not trust the process at all.

2. Is your school *dating* PLCs? We will identify statements, practices, and habits that are common among schools dating the PLC process. By *dating*, we mean schools that exhibit many of the same characteristics, but are further along than schools that are still flirting with the process. They, too, eventually stall if they don't move on from dating. These schools often develop the products associated with PLCs, but they don't attain the student learning results they expect. These schools have moved beyond wondering about the process. They've taken some action but have not done what's needed for deep commitment. Because of this, there's always the risk of a breakup.

3. Is your school *engaged* to PLCs? We will identify statements, practices, and habits of mind that are common among schools engaged in the PLC process. By *engaged*, we mean schools that have made the commitments necessary for deep implementation—schools that have "put a ring on it." These schools have established a culture of collective responsibility and use their vision (strengthened in the Eye stage) as their primary focus. They develop the products associated with

PLCs, and see the student learning results they expect. These schools use authentic alignment to deepen collective responsibility in a PLC.

Your goal in this step is to honestly reflect on and assess your school's or team's progress with essential PLC work. You may find that you have done great work so far that deserves validation; likewise, as with any ongoing journey, you will also find areas that you should revamp, revise, or revisit. It is not our intention here to provide a step-by-step guide on how to implement each area of the essential work of a PLC. Rather, we think this step in the authentic alignment process bonds—like Velcro—your mission and vision work and your essential efforts to support PLC implementation. Next we'll look at the difference between cultures of *learning for some* and *learning for all* in the context of this essential work.

Creating a Collaborative Culture in a PLC

In order to ensure all students learn, educators must work collaboratively rather than in isolation and take collective responsibility for student learning. The collaborative team must replace the isolated classroom as the fundamental structure of the school. Collaborative teams are the engines that drive the organization's efforts to achieve its mission of high levels of learning for all students.

Educators today have access to more information, strategies, instructional practices, and teacher knowledge than at any other point in history. PLCs that focus on collective inquiry take advantage of these resources to relentlessly pursue the best outcomes for all students and to challenge existing practices that may no longer be yielding desired results.

Every teacher reaches a crossroads when he or she has tried every known strategy, intervention, and instructional idea in his or her teaching arsenal to reach a student—when, in spite of these efforts, a student remains less than successful. In a culture in which we believe only some students can learn at high levels, this teacher might conclude that there should be some acceptable and expected level of failure for some. In a culture of collective responsibility, this teacher would have access to systems that afforded opportunities to collaborate with peers in an effort to find a structural breakthrough. Embedding systems in which teacher teams engage in building shared knowledge of best practice is aligned with a culture of learning for all.

Capitalizing on the collective expertise of others in a collaborative culture helps to improve teacher efficacy and confidence. When teachers know there is an embedded system of teacher support available on a consistent basis, it increases the prospect of accessing answers that result in breakthroughs much more than teaching in isolation.

Working in a collaborative culture represents a shift from making excuses to being empowered. We liken this difference to that between a thermometer and a thermostat. Thermometer teachers take the temperature of their classrooms. In other words, the level of success for students greatly depends on what they bring to the table. Even our best teachers can only do so much working in isolation, and therefore they naturally become dependent on other factors for student success. Thermostat teams, on the other hand, set the temperature of the room. They implement systems to ensure that frequent, effective collaboration yields many ideas, resources, strategies, and possibilities, that the team feels confident in its ability to ensure learning for all—regardless of who their students are, where they're from, and who their parents are or are not. (To read more about building a collaborative culture, we suggest referring to *Learning by Doing* [DuFour et al., 2010a] and *Transforming School Culture* [Muhammad, 2009]).

To assess your team's progress in building a collaborative culture— are you dating it, flirting with it, or engaged to it?—use the following rating scale (see figure 5.1) to indicate which statements are true of your team. This scale is adapted from the work of DuFour, DuFour, Eaker, and Many (2010a).

First, complete the survey in figure 5.1 individually. For items that are true, cite evidence to support your claim. Then share and discuss the results and use the data to plan your next steps as a team.

Actions for Flirting With a PLC	Yes	No	As Evidenced By . . .
1. The responsibility of creating time for collaboration is left to individuals, or created in the master schedule for some, but not all.			
2. Specialists—such as fine arts teachers, related arts teachers, elective teachers, and media specialists—are left twisting in the wind with regard to being members of a team.			
3. We believe we are a PLC because "we did a book study" or because "we have a weekly meeting for an hour."			
4. We are invited to collaborate, but not expected to collaborate.			
5. We meet because the principal requires us to meet.			
6. With regard to our meetings, if given a choice, we could take them or leave them.			
7. During our PLC meetings, we think about the other things we could be doing at that time.			
8. One person on our team wrote the norms, and the rest of us agreed to them.			
9. We seem to talk about everything except student learning at our team meeting.			

Continued on next page ↓

Figure 5.1: Chart for rating progress on building collaborative culture in your PLC: —Flirting, dating, or being engaged?

Actions for Flirting With a PLC (continued)	Yes	No	As Evidenced By . . .
10. We don't think we need a weekly meeting to collaborate; we collaborate all the time in the hallway, during transitions, and sometimes at lunch. We have so many informal meetings that we don't see the need to sit down at a set time . . . and you should see the number of emails we exchange!			
11. Some teachers and some teams are allowed to opt out of collaboration.			
12. Teams set compliance goals—by taking out last year's goals, changing a couple of the numbers, and updating the school year.			

Actions for Dating a PLC	Yes	No	As Evidenced By . . .
1. The responsibility of ensuring collaboration is left to team leaders, team facilitators, or instructional coaches.			
2. We are encouraged to collaborate, but not expected to collaborate.			
3. Time for collaboration is built into the master schedule, but administrators sometimes interfere with that time with other priorities.			
4. We have a PLC coach who runs our meeting.			
5. Our norms were developed for us, and handed to us by our principal.			

Actions for Dating a PLC (continued)	Yes	No	As Evidenced By . . .
6. We do not have an agreed-on process for holding one another accountable for honoring our norms.			
7. We developed team norms, but when someone violates one of the norms, no one confronts him or her about it.			
8. We are a PLC because we complete an agenda after every meeting.			

Actions for Being Engaged to a PLC*	Yes	No	As Evidenced By . . .
1. Teams are created on the basis of shared responsibility for pursuing the critical questions of teaching and learning with a particular group of students: for example, by course or by grade level.			
2. Leaders work with us to find creative ways to provide more time for team collaboration, including ways of using existing time more effectively.			
3. Leadership is dispersed more widely by identifying team leaders for any team with more than three people. We meet with team leaders on a regular basis to identify problematic areas of the process, and develop strategies for resolving those problems.			
4. Building shared knowledge of best practice is part of the process of shared decision making at both the school and team level.			
5. Teams are asked to build shared knowledge—to learn together as we approach each new task in the collaborative process.			

Continued on next page ↓

Actions for Being Engaged to a PLC (continued)	Yes	No	As Evidenced By . . .
6. Supporting research, templates, exemplars, worksheets, and timelines are available to teams to assist us in each step of the process.			
7. Each team monitors our ongoing progress and assesses our products, regularly meets with team leaders, and does formal self-evaluations. Leaders respond immediately to a team that is having difficulty. Teams celebrate and use as a model the teams who are experiencing success.			
8. Building-level leadership teams model everything being asked of collaborative teams, including meeting on a regular basis, staying focused on issues with the greatest impact on student achievement, establishing and honoring collective commitments, and working toward established goals.			
9. We work together interdependently to achieve common goals, but this does not mean there is no room for individual skill, thought, or effort. In fact, these elements are strengthened by a collaborative culture.			
10. Teacher collaboration has two purposes: for individuals to become better teachers, and to help others become better teachers. One of those two things is always happening when we're meeting as a collaborative team.			
11. Procedures are created to ensure teams are able to learn from one another.			
12. Teams are the focus of recognition and celebration. Leaders take every opportunity to acknowledge the efforts and accomplishments of teams.			

Source: DuFour et al., 2010a, pp. 149–150.

Visit go.solution-tree.com/plcbooks for a reproducible version of this figure.

Clearly Defining What Every Student Must Learn

In determining what we want our students to learn, a natural first step is to prioritize essential learning standards. Robert J. Marzano, John S. Kendall, and Barbara B. Gaddy (1999) suggest that if educators want to cover all of the standards currently in curriculum guides, they "would have to change schooling from K–12 to K–22" (p. 5). Clearly this is not an option that schools or districts can accommodate, nor is it desirable from a practical schooling sense. Douglas Reeves (2004), who introduced the notion of power standards to the education community with his book *Accountability in Action*, recognizes the challenges educators face "because of the limitations of time and the extraordinary variety in learning backgrounds of students, teachers, and leaders." He states that educators "need focus and clarity in order to prepare their students for success" (p. 167). He suggests that three criteria—endurance, leverage, and readiness for the next level of learning—be employed in priority determinations. The notion of *endurance* involves those concepts or skills that remain with the learner long after the test. Think about the skills you learned in school that are applicable in your life as an adult. *Leverage* concerns those concepts or skills that appear in more than one curricular area. *Readiness for the next level of learning* is a reminder to educators that vertical alignment with the grade level above and below is an important consideration. Larry Ainsworth (2013) also reminds us that establishing priority standards does not mean that the remaining standards are not taught. He makes the point using the metaphor of a fence:

> Like fence *posts*, Priority Standards provide curricular focus in which teachers need to "dig deeper" and ensure student competency. Like fence *rails*, supporting standards are curricular standards that *connect to and support* the Priority Standards. Without both the posts and the rails, there can be no fence. (p. 18)

Ken had the honor of leading some professional development with renowned educator and national PLC expert Tim Brown in Memphis, Tennessee. He listened to Tim speak of the importance of clarity about what every student needs to learn. Tim shared a protocol for identifying essential learning standards with teachers and administrators. In the middle of explaining the logistics of the protocol, he stopped and made the following statement: "Remember, essential standards are not merely a list to be developed, but a list of promises made to students" (Tim Brown, personal communication, May 28, 2013). This poignant statement has remained a focus of our work with educators ever since.

Educators must come together to establish a clear and consistent direction as well as targets for student learning. Teams must take the time to identify the need to knows versus the nice to knows. (To read more about clarity on what every student must learn, see *Learning by Doing* [DuFour et al., 2010a] and *Common Formative Assessment: A Toolkit for Professional Learning Communities at Work* [Bailey & Jakicic, 2012].)

To assess your team's progress in defining what every student must learn—whether you're dating it, flirting with it, or engaged to it—use the following rating scale (see figure 5.2) to indicate which statements are true of your team. This scale is adapted from the work of DuFour, DuFour, Eaker, and Many (2010a).

First, complete the survey in figure 5.2 individually. For items that are true, cite evidence to support your claim. Then share and discuss the results and use the data to plan your next steps as a team.

Consider the following scenario. Three outstanding teachers sit facing one another with a list of what they believe are the eight most important targets for ninth-grade mathematics students to learn in the first quarter of the school year. Their lists are based on evidence, research, and experience. You would sleep easily every night knowing that any one of these three teachers was responsible for your child learning mathematics. And yet, when they sat down and compared their lists, to their amazement, they produced three different lists. So what happens if there is no collaboration after this

Actions for Flirting With a PLC	Yes	No	As Evidenced By . . .
1. We think selecting essential targets feels like one more thing to do—to check off the PLC list.			
2. We don't see this step as necessary, as the district has already identified the most important targets in our curriculum. They're the ones in bold print!			
3. When we are asked to complete an activity, we aren't exactly sure how it is connected to the overall PLC process.			
4. The idea of prioritizing standards sounds good initially, but we are not sure it's worth the potential conflict that might arise from the differing opinions of our teammates.			
Actions for Dating a PLC	**Yes**	**No**	**As Evidenced By . . .**
1. We have essential learning targets, but we don't really monitor how our students are progressing toward mastery.			
2. We have essential learning targets, but deciding what's most important is still left to the discretion of the individual teacher.			

Continued on next page ↓

Figure 5.2: Chart for rating progress on defining what every student must learn: —Flirting, dating, or being engaged?

Actions for Dating a PLC (continued)	Yes	No	As Evidenced By . . .
3. We inform students of the targets, but they don't receive support to reach them.			
4. We display the essential targets in the classroom so the principal can see them during walkthroughs.			
5. We don't hold students who are performing years below grade level to the essential grade-level standards.			

Actions for Being Engaged to a PLC*	Yes	No	As Evidenced By . . .
1. We understand that less is more; "the main problem with curricula in North America is not that we do not have enough, but rather that we attempt to do too much" (DuFour et al., 2010a, p. 86).			
2. We identify the most essential targets. Every team is engaged in a process to clarify exactly what each student is to learn in each grade level, course, and unit of instruction.			
3. We focus on mastery, not coverage. Not all standards are of equal importance. By focusing on the essential skills, teachers prepare students for 80 to 90 percent of the content that will be addressed on state and provincial tests and provide them with the reading, writing, and reasoning skills to address any question that could appear (Reeves, 2002, as cited in DuFour et al., 2010a, p. 86).			

Actions for Being Engaged to a PLC (continued)	Yes	No	As Evidenced By . . .
4. We expose all students to the grade-level essential standards. All students—even those currently working below grade level—must know the standard and have it as a goal. We as educators must problem solve as a team about how to best and most efficiently fill the gap between where students are and where they need to be.			
5. We know that the power is in the collaborative process of identifying the essential targets, not simply in generating the list.			
6. We set short-term SMART goals that are specific, measurable, attainable, results oriented, and time bound. Educators use the mastery of identified standards as powerful, practical, and motivating short-term team SMART goals.			
7. We use, review, and rewrite. The process of deciding what is most important to teach is not over after teams identify essential standards because we must then use them and reflect on them for a period of time to ensure we selected the correct standards (Bailey & Jakicic, 2012).			

Source: DuFour et al., 2010a.

Visit go.solution-tree.com/plcbooks for a reproducible version of this figure.

point? Here we have three great individual teachers, but they will never be a great team, and they will send three groups of ninth-grade students to tenth grade who are prepared differently. And the tenth-grade mathematics teachers will then face students of varying strengths and levels of preparedness, and they will spend precious time filling gaps among all three groups of students before they can begin tenth-grade instruction. This example shows how important it is to change the paradigm.

Constantly Measuring Effectiveness

We have to challenge educators to think about their assessment practice and how they derive information about student progress. If the purpose of assessment is merely to rank and sort, then little needs to change from the assessment practices of previous generations. If the purpose is a focus on student learning, then educators need to examine whether their current practice is aligned with that outcome. Tom Hierck (2009) suggests that for seamless assessment and instruction in the ongoing information exchange between teacher and student, the teacher's role is to "make frequent environmental scans to collect formal evidence such as assessments, exams, or homework, and informal evidence such as the questions students may ask, their comments during group work, or even their confused expressions" (p. 252). Analysis of this evidence allows educators to plan next steps and adjust instruction going forward.

It is not our intent to debate the merits of summative versus formative assessment. Current educational practice involves *summative assessment* (assessment *of* learning). We recognize the need for a balanced approach to assessment but strongly advocate effective *formative assessment* (assessment *for* learning) that scaffolds student learning up to the expectations of the summative test. As Michael Fullan (2005) notes, "Assessment for learning . . . when done well, is one of the most powerful high-leverage strategies for improving student learning that we know of" (p. 71).

Developing and improving formative assessment practice and engaging with colleagues in the process (from writing to analyzing) of common formative assessments are high-yield strategies that positively impact student learning. When you gather and analyze data from common formative assessments, then you monitor the effectiveness of your assessment practice. This further aligns you with the positive outcomes of student learning and helps students understand that assessment is a part of the learning process.

Teams within a PLC must change the way they use assessments—it's not enough to take a grade and then sort students to receive intervention. Each teacher must use the evidence of student learning to collaborate with colleagues to identify either teaching strengths to share or areas of concern for which to seek new instructional strategies. Again, in a culture of collective responsibility, teams address learning for all and take responsibility to ensure it; their collective knowledge means schoolwide student learning breakthroughs. Collaborative teams use evidence of student learning to identify the knowledge, skills, and dispositions that many students find problematic. This evidence drives professional learning and action research to support more effective teaching of the curriculum.

While all this sounds evident, it's one of the most neglected areas in this essential work. Teachers sometimes avoid the idea of taking instructional action on data from common formative assessment analysis. Every team should engage in a process to assess student learning on a timely and frequent basis through the use of teacher-developed common formative assessments. Let's explore what it looks like when schools develop products and don't get results as well as when they produce meaningful results. (To learn more about constantly measuring your effectiveness, see *Learning by Doing* [DuFour et al., 2010a] and *Common Formative Assessment: A Toolkit for Professional Learning Communities at Work* [Bailey & Jakicic, 2012].)

To assess your team's progress with constantly rating effectiveness—whether you're dating it, flirting with it, or engaged to it—use the following rating scale (see figure 5.3) to indicate which statements are true of your team. This scale is adapted from the work of DuFour, DuFour, Eaker, and Many (2010a).

First, complete the survey in figure 5.3 individually. For items that are true, cite evidence to support your claim. Then share and discuss the results and use the data to plan your next steps as a team.

When you understand the Why and How, then this shift in how you work and in how you analyze and use data begins to make sense. Table 5.1 (page 115) describes this shift.

Common assessment data are only effective when they're instructionally actionable. It's no longer acceptable to limit assessment analysis to determining *what's wrong with students.* In our work with teachers, we often ask them to finish this sentence: "Common formative assessments are considered assessments ____ _____." In unison, they respond, "for learning." Yet when we check for fidelity, teachers often don't reach the point where they learn from the assessment. Assessment for learning is often interpreted as *assessment for learning what students know and what they don't know.* The fact is that when it comes to meeting the needs of students, assessment for learning means finding out what students *and* teachers know and don't know. This is an important point of emphasis.

Common formative assessments are not meant to identify "good" teachers or "bad" teachers; they are designed to help you fulfill the moral imperative of learning for all. So if your students this year aren't mastering mixed fractions at the pace and level of success as your students last year, you mustn't just conclude that this year's students aren't as capable. The effective use of common formative assessment data in a collaborative culture should provide additional strategies, tips, and insights to help students bridge the gap between current performance and mastery of the essential standard. You engage in the kind of dialogue and problem solving that can result in additional tools and strategies to meet the needs of this year's students. When this happens, students obviously benefit from it, and teachers, who are clearly capable based on last year's results, continue to improve.

Actions for Flirting With a PLC	Yes	No	As Evidenced By . . .
1. We use the assessments that come with the textbook series as our common formative assessments.			
2. Our principal requires us to do a common assessment every week. Before we can get the first assessment scored, the next one is due to be administered.			
3. Our team feels like we are "pushing paper" when doing common assessments.			
4. On our team, we ask our strongest teachers to create the assessment, and the rest of us just go along with it.			.
5. We create common formative assessments during the summer, and they're still on our shelf.			
6. We don't see the point in comparing assessment data for instructional effectiveness. We are all professionals, and the students we serve are different.			
7. Our students are grouped by ability. Comparing instructional effectiveness on these common formative assessments is demoralizing.			

Continued on next page ↓

Figure 5.3: Chart for assessing progress on constantly rating effectiveness: —Flirting, dating, or being engaged?

Actions for Flirting With a PLC (continued)	Yes	No	As Evidenced By . . .
8. We're doing common formative assessments, though there wasn't a lot of explanation or guidance given.			
9. My team gives common formative assessments because my principal requires us to.			
10. I don't get what makes a common formative assessment different from any other assessment. It's a new buzzword.			

Actions for Dating a PLC	Yes	No	As Evidenced By . . .
1. We do common assessments on our team. Someone else should score them.			
2. We do common assessments on our team. Someone else does score them.			
3. We never seem to get any further than examining the data to see how students performed.			
4. Our team isn't ready to talk about teacher effectiveness using common formative assessment data.			
5. We definitely use common formative assessment data as a grade. If we don't grade these assessments, our students will not take them seriously.			
6. Some teams opt to use common formative assessments, while other teams don't have to give them.			

Actions for Dating a PLC (continued)	Yes	No	As Evidenced By . . .
7. Our principal has not communicated expectations regarding common formative assessments.			
8. We wish we did more with the data gathered from common formative assessments.			
9. We don't compare data with each other for fear that it will reflect negatively on our evaluations.			

Actions for Being Engaged to a PLC*	Yes	No	As Evidenced By . . .
1. We know that it's what teams do with data that matters. We translate data into information because "data alone will not help individuals or teams improve. They need the context of valid comparison to satisfy strengths and weaknesses." (DuFour et al., 2010a, p. 200)			
2. We make sure that every teacher receives frequent and timely information regarding his or her students' success in learning the essential curriculum. We then use that information to identify strengths and weaknesses as part of a process of continuous improvement.			
3. We use apples-to-apples comparisons. "Comparisons are most informative when conditions are similar. . . Equivalent situations yield the most meaningful comparisons" (DuFour et al., 2010a, p. 200).			
4. We calibrate scoring of student work. "Every team is engaged in a process to clarify consistent criteria by which to assess the quality of student work" (DuFour et al., 2008, pp. 116–117).			

Continued on next page ↓

Actions for Being Engaged to a PLC (continued)	Yes	No	As Evidenced By . . .
5. We use balanced assessments. "No one source yields the comprehensive results necessary to inform and improve practice." We use "different types of formative assessments based on the knowledge or skills students are called upon to demonstrate rather than relying exclusively on one type of assessment—multiple-choice tests, performance-based assessments, constructed-response tests, and so on." We attempt to determine the best evidence of student learning and the most effective ways to gather that evidence. We develop multiple ways for students to demonstrate proficiency. (DuFour et al. 2010a, pp. 200–201)			
6. We use a protocol for analyzing assessment data. A protocol specifically designed for common formative assessment analysis ensures that we honor every stage of the process. It structures the conversation around student work so that each team member has time to speak and everyone else has time to listen. We keep presenting, examining, questioning, and responding in balance so that the meeting moves optimally and is honest and respectful (McDonald, Mohr, Dichter, & McDonald, 2007, as cited in DuFour et al., 2010a).			
7. We have a fixation with results that does not mean inattention to people. PLCs are committed to both results and relationships as they recognize that the best way to achieve a culture of collective responsibility is through collaborative relationships that foster ongoing growth and development (DuFour et al., 2010a).			
8. We collect instructionally actionable common assessment data so we can be ready to act on them.			

Source: DuFour et al., 2010a, pp. 116–117, 200–201.

*Visit **go.solution-tree.com/plcbooks** for a reproducible version of this figure.*

Table 5.1: Shifting From an Old Way of Using Data to a New Paradigm

Old Paradigm	New Paradigm
Using data to evaluate and assign a grade	Using data to inform instructional practices
Using data to identify what is right or wrong with students	Using data to compare instructional effectiveness between teachers
Using data to help students learn more	Using data to help students *and* teachers learn more

If you've been teaching for more than two years, then you have experienced the very humbling phenomenon of roller coaster results from one year to the next. In a culture of collective responsibility, instead of placing the burden of expected achievement on uncontrollable factors, staff focus on the collective expertise of the people inside the school. They are willing to sacrifice traditional norms of teacher isolation and embrace the powerful synergy of effective collaboration. They understand, welcome, and embrace the challenge of ensuring high levels of learning for every student. They no longer analyze common assessment data out of compliance. They see the process of engaging in this type of dialogue as part of the promise their school has made to students, parents, and staff. This represents a very powerful transition from doing PLCs to becoming a PLC.

Systematically Responding When Students Do or Do Not Learn

Consider this common situation in schools: a teacher decides that ten questions are required to demonstrate student knowledge of a topic. Some students answer these questions in the allotted time and are deemed proficient. There are also some students who complete the questions with time to spare. Their reward is more of the same.

They are given additional questions, teaching them the lesson of time management (work slower next time) but little else. Some students answer only four questions. They take the test again with the same result. How long will it take for the teacher to notice they don't understand? This is especially true for English learners—teachers try again, but slower and louder. The response to this hypothetical situation really gets to the core of what schools believe is their focus on learning. Is learning left to chance? Is it different from class to class and dependent on the teacher? Do students have to win the teacher lottery to get the best results? Or is learning intentional and the promise of learning for all is, in fact, more than words on a poster? Do you have protected time during the school day to reteach and enrich students? Schools that make student learning their fundamental purpose spend a great deal of time in conversation about enrichment and intervention and recognize that these factors are within the purview of all teachers (DuFour et al., 2010a).

One of the common challenges of implementing a system to respond when students do and do not learn occurs when response to intervention (RTI) becomes a support almost separate and apart from the other essential work of a PLC. RTI can best be understood as the teacher practices (instructional delivery, assessment, and student discipline) and typical processes (the daily, weekly, or monthly routines of educators, such as schedules, collaborative times, and methods of communicating) that impact and are impacted by the things we do in education. It's about using the knowledge, skills, and attributes of the members of a learning organization to positively impact the outcomes for all students. RTI should be embedded in a culture of collective responsibility. Mike Mattos, one of the architects of the RTI at Work™ process, once remarked in a keynote presentation that most schools don't have an RTI problem—they have a "first best instruction" problem. At many schools struggling to establish a culture of collective responsibility in a PLC, RTI eventually becomes the place where we send students.

Another challenge schools experience is when they are, as we have described, just flirting with or dating the essential work of a PLC. When this is the case, the number of students who slip through the cracks and find themselves in need of intervention support simply overwhelms the RTI system. Greater fidelity to the promise of PLCs means you can identify the learning needs of many of those students earlier in the process. In PLCs, the school has a systematic plan to ensure students receive additional time and support for learning; this means that the school can make the following pledge to every student and parent: "It does not matter which teacher you have in our school; if you need extra help to learn at high levels, we guarantee you will receive it." (To learn more, see *Learning by Doing* [DuFour et al., 2010a], *Simplifying Response to Intervention* [Buffum et al., 2012], and *Pyramid of Behavior Interventions: Seven Keys to a Positive Learning Environment* [Hierck, Coleman, & Weber, 2011].)

To assess your team's progress with systematically responding when students do and don't learn—whether you're dating it, flirting with it, or engaged to it—use the following rating scale (see figure 5.4, pages 118–120; adapted from the work of DuFour, DuFour, Eaker, and Many, 2010a) to indicate which statements are true of your team.

First, complete the survey in figure 5.4 individually. For items that are true, cite evidence to support your claim. Then share and discuss the results and use the data to plan your next steps as a team.

Clarifying Shared Collective Commitments

By this point, your teams should be clear on the differences between doing PLCs and being a PLC, and among flirting with, dating, and being engaged to the process. Now it's time to clarify your shared collective commitments.

Use figure 5.5 (pages 122–124) to review each shared collective commitment categorized under the essential work of a PLC. This scale is adapted from the work of DuFour, DuFour, Eaker, and Many (2010a). First, consider the Why—are you clear on why this

Actions for Flirting With a PLC	Yes	No	As Evidenced By . . .
1. We can't fit RTI into our school schedule, so after-school tutoring is our best option. Of course, the students who need it the most don't always show up.			
2. We use RTI primarily to identify students for special education services.			
3. Our grading practices make intervention opportunities not worth pursuing.			
4. We taught it. They didn't get it. So we let the intervention people deal with it.			
5. Our students get RTI time during specials and electives.			
6. We have not designated an intervention block or time in the master schedule for RTI.			.

Actions for Dating a PLC	Yes	No	As Evidenced By . . .
1. Our RTI model is great because it's a place where I can send students who are struggling to learn.			
2. Our RTI model focuses on our bubble students (those who are close to proficient).			
3. We "do" RTI, but we can't tell you if it's really working.			
4. We "do" RTI, but we don't have a comprehensive implementation plan.			
5. RTI at our school has more to do with adult paperwork than it does with helping students learn.			
6. At our school, we pull students out of math to get them caught up in math.			

Actions for Dating a PLC (continued)	Yes	No	As Evidenced By . . .
7. RTI helps our school see what's wrong with the student.			
8. We focus many resources on administering and collecting assessment data rather than on helping staff learn to use the data.			

Actions for Being Engaged to a PLC*	Yes	No	As Evidenced By . . .
1. We use evidence of student learning to identify students, by name and by need, by student and by standard, who require additional time and support for learning.			
2. We believe that no support system will compensate for bad teaching. "Schools characterized by weak and ineffective teaching will not solve their problems by creating a system of timely interventions for students. Eventually, that system will be crushed by the weight of the mass of students it's attempting to support (DuFour et al., 2010a, p. 111–112)."			
3. We use timely interventions. A student should not have to fail for months, quarters, semesters, or until state test results return in the fall to receive additional support. At least every three to four weeks there should be a systematic process to identify students in need of additional support.			
4. We use directive interventions. If the school's fundamental purpose is to ensure that all students learn, then students cannot be given the option of failure. A learning-focused school will not accept the narrative of "It is our job to teach, and the student's job to learn," or "We are preparing students for the real world, so requiring them to get help is enabling and will not teach them responsibility."			

Figure 5.4: Chart for rating our effectiveness on systematically responding when students do and don't learn: —Flirting, dating, or being engaged?

Continued on next page →

Actions for Being Engaged to a PLC (continued)	Yes	No	As Evidenced By . . .
5. We use an intervention model that reflects the unique context of our school. Schools should create their own plans rather than adopting the program of another school. The value is in the process, not simply mimicking an existing program from another school.			
6. We have a plan for enrichment. Every school has a specific plan to enrich and extend the learning of students who are not challenged by the required curriculum.			
7. We realize that more of the same is not effective intervention. Effective intervention is characterized by differentiation and precision. Intervention offers a setting and strategies that are different from those already proven to be ineffective for the student. An intervention system that only reports a student is failing in a subject will not be as effective as a system that can identify the specific skill or skills that are causing the student difficulty.			
8. We make sure students in need of additional support are never pulled from new direct instruction. Interventions must be in addition to core instruction—not in place of it. Pulling students from essential grade-level curriculum and replacing it with below-grade-level coursework is not an intervention—it is glorified tracking. The lowest-performing students will never catch up. Students taught below grade level every day will end up below grade level. To achieve the goal of additional support without pullout, the school will create flexible time in the master schedule to provide interventions during the school day. Every school must have a specific plan to ensure that students who experience initial difficulty in learning are provided with additional time and support for learning during the school day in a timely and directive way that does not cause the student to miss any new direct instruction.			

Source: DuFour et al., 2010a, pp. 111–112.

*Visit **go.solution-tree.com/plcbooks** for a reproducible version of this figure.*

collective commitment is aligned with a school with a commitment to learning for all? Then consider the How—are you clear on the process associated with the commitment? If you require support in either of these first two areas, check the Question column. After you have considered the Why and the How, or gained clarity on the question you had, place your initials in the final column, indicating your investment in the collective commitment.

Elevating All Students

The staff at many schools assert their belief that all students can learn. Their shared mission and vision reflect this belief; however, it's not always aligned with their daily work. This disconnect drives the How stage of authentic alignment. The behaviors that shape your day-to-day work of teaching and leading should embody your school's mission and vision as shaped by the Why and the Eye. As you work to increase investment in your collective commitments, you must do more than simply consider misaligned behaviors as compliance issues. You must invest in the shared collective commitments you've identified as best practices to help your school live its mission and vision. Leaders must go beneath the surface to understand why certain behaviors permeate a school culture, and it's important to discuss within your teams the connection between these high-leverage best practices and your school's shared mission and vision.

Learning for all means you'll do whatever it takes to make that so—not by lowering your standards, but by elevating all students to reach them. The final stage of authentic alignment, integrating or the Now, provides strategies to help you modify and redirect existing aspects of school life in a way that centers what's most important in everything you do.

Collective Commitment	Why	How	Question	Initial
In order to promote a collaborative culture . . .				
I will contribute to identifying team norms and protocols to guide us in working together.				
I commit to analyzing student achievement data and establishing SMART goals that my team works interdependently to achieve.				
I commit to evaluating our adherence to and the effectiveness of our team norms at least twice each year.				
In order to get clear on what every student needs to learn . . .				
I commit to clarifying the most important essential learnings of each course with my team. These targets are aligned with state, district, or provincial assessments required of our students.				
I promise to align the essential learnings with state and district standards and the high-stakes exams required of our students.				
I commit to identifying course content or topics that can be eliminated so our team can devote more time to the essential curriculum.				
I agree to contribute to a process for sequencing the content of the course and have established pacing guides to help students achieve the intended essential learnings.				

Collective Commitment	Why	How	Question	Initial
I commit to identifying the prerequisite knowledge and skills students need in order to master the essential learnings of our courses and each of their units.				
I commit to teach the agreed-upon and guaranteed and viable curriculum.				
In order to constantly measure my effectiveness . . .				
I commit to developing team-created and frequent common formative assessments that help my team determine each student's mastery of essential learnings.				
I commit to developing team-created and frequent common formative assessments that help my team to determine which of our instructional practices were most effective.				
I commit to establishing the proficiency standard we want each student to achieve on each skill and concept that our common formative assessments examine.				
I commit to develop common summative assessments that help our team assess the strengths and weaknesses of our instruction.				
I commit to establishing the proficiency standard we want each student to achieve on each skill and concept that our summative assessments examine.				

Continued on next page →

Figure 5.5: Review exercise for shared collective commitments for the essential work of a PLC.

Collective Commitment	Why	How	Question	Initial
I commit to helping establish the criteria our team will use to judge the quality of student work related to the essential learnings of our course and practice applying those criteria to ensure consistency.				
I commit to teaching students the criteria we will use in judging the quality of their work and providing them with examples.				
I commit to use the results of our common assessments to assist others in building strengths and addressing weaknesses as part of a process of continuous improvement designed to help students learn at higher levels.				
In order to systematically respond when students do and don't learn . . .				
I commit to using the results of our common assessments to identify students who need additional time and support to master essential learning and working within the systems and processes of the school to ensure they receive that support.				
I commit to taking interventions above and beyond what all students receive. I won't call for students to be pulled out of core subjects to be caught up in that same core subject.				
I commit to gather evidence of student learning, share it with my colleagues, and use that evidence to inform and improve my instructional practice.				

Source: DuFour et al., 2010a, pp. 130–131.

Visit go.solution-tree.com/plcbooks for a reproducible version of this figure.

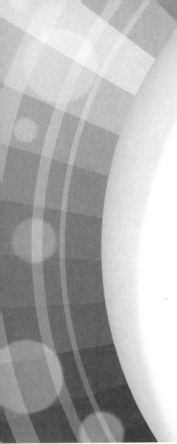

Chapter 6

Integrating: The Now

A culture is made—or destroyed—by its articulate voices.

—AYN RAND

Integrating, the Now, is a process for embedding your shared mission (examined in the Why), your vision (explored in the Eye), and your collective commitments for best practice (outlined in the How) into existing school structures to ensure your school operates as a PLC and soars rather than stalls. This step strengthens the fourth foundational pillar of your PLC: goals.

Maintaining alignment and managing your culture is a process, not an event; it never ends. We know leaders who have grown quite frustrated over their inability to change the culture of their organizations and center what is most important in everything they do. That frustration often stems from focusing on accountability, testing, and scores rather than concentrating on shared mission, vision, and values. Schools might also lack the tools essential to connect their cultures to their structures. Without these connections among mission and vision and daily practice, the work does not take hold. A culture of excuse making dominates.

The Now stage asks you to reflect on and consider critical issues for strengthening your goals pillar. You will find guiding questions that:

1. Provide clarity about and understanding of the connection between collective commitments and shared mission

2. Help you align structure and resources for practical application of collective commitments

The Now stage supports you as you move from inspiration and aspiration to the practical. You will think about how to create, embed, and align structures that support your culture of collective responsibility. You will consider how to put your shared mission and vision into action. And you will envision what your school can do to intentionally connect the Why to the work.

- How do we / will we organize people into teams to support collaboration?

- How do we / will we provide time for collaboration?

- How do we / will we create a guaranteed and viable curriculum?

- How do we / will we monitor each student's learning?

- How do we / will we ensure that students who struggle receive additional time and support for learning that are timely, diagnostic, directive, and systematic?

- How do we / will we enrich the learning for students who are highly proficient?

- How do we / will we use evidence of student learning to improve our practice?

- How do we / will we know if we are making progress toward becoming the school we seek to become? What targets and timelines have we established? Have we established any SMART goals?

Reciprocal Accountability

In chapter 4, you envisioned the critical issues when you identified areas where you needed to build shared knowledge. In the Now, we revisit them through a different lens, the lens of reciprocal accountability. DuFour et al. (2010) remind us that when school leaders call upon others to engage in new work, achieve new standards, and accomplish new goals, they have a responsibility to develop the capacity of those they lead to be successful in meeting these challenges. Richard Elmore (2004) refers to this relationship as *reciprocal accountability*:

> For every increment of performance I demand from you, I have an equal responsibility to provide you with the capacity to meet that expectation. Likewise, for every investment you make in my skill and knowledge, I have a reciprocal responsibility to demonstrate some new increment in performance (p. 93).

It's not enough for leaders to communicate clear expectations. They have to both make clear what's expected, and then provide the resources, support, and develop the capacity of staff to achieve the expectations. For years, when Ken was asked to describe his job as a principal, he would respond, "My job is four-fold. . . . I hunt, gather, protect, and defend!"

- Hunt and gather all the resources and supports necessary for collaborative teams to engage in the right work, the right way
- Protect the agreed-upon collective commitments by reinforcing aligned behaviors and confronting misaligned behaviors
- Defend the school's shared mission and shared vision by reinforcing a culture that examines every decision through the lens of supporting high levels of learning for all students

One of the objectives in the Now is to address the very common ambiguity that often stalls teams when they are in the process of PLC transformation. As teams begin to think about next steps or what now, DuFour et al., (2010a, p. 2) remind us of some of these questions to address:

- **Why questions.** Why should we do this? Can you present a rationale as to why we should engage in this work? Is there evidence that suggests the outcome of this work is desirable, feasible, and more effective than what we have traditionally done?

- **What questions.** What are the exact meanings of key terms? What resources, tools, templates, materials, and examples can you provide to assist in our work?

- **How questions.** How do we proceed? How do you propose we do this? Is there a preferred process?

- **When questions.** When will we find time to do this? When do you expect us to complete the task? What is the timeline?

- **Guiding questions.** Which questions are we attempting to answer? Which questions will help us stay focused on the right work?

- **Quality questions.** What criteria will be used to judge the quality of our work? What criteria can we use to assess our own work?

- **Assurance questions.** What suggestions can you offer to increase the likelihood of our success? What cautions can you alert us to? Where do we turn when we struggle?

Aligning With Collective Commitments and Core Values

In the How chapter, we identified the essential work required to build a culture of collective responsibility in a PLC (DuFour et al., 2010a):

1. A focus on learning
2. A collaborative culture

3. Defining what every student must learn

4. Constantly measuring effectiveness

5. Systematically responding when students do and do not learn

In the Now stage, it is time for you to reflect on how the essential work breaks down into specific structures and day-to-day tasks of leaders and teams in your culture of collective responsibility. The Now involves considering what you must do to answer the following questions.

1. How do we create a focus on learning?

2. How do we build, support, and nurture a culture of collaboration?

3. How do we get clear on what every student must learn?

4. How do we constantly measure students' effectiveness?

5. How do we systematically respond when students do and do not learn?

Depending on where your school or team is on the PLC journey, you may find that you already have areas in which your PLC implementation is strong and other areas where it is weaker. Regardless, we hope the Now stage illuminates opportunities for growth. We caution you to really go beneath the surface of the issues you will examine in this chapter. The most valuable part—the gold—in the activities that follow comes not with simply completing a chart, but rather in the dialogue that surfaces as you engage in honest reflective assessment.

Critical Issues for Team Consideration

Working in teams, examine each of the critical issues in figure 6.1 (developed by Tim Brown, pages 131–135) and do three things.

1. Indicate using the scale provided the extent to which each issue is true of your team. Be sure to discuss the rationale behind each rating.

2. Brainstorm ways in which the principal might provide teams with the structure and support to be successful in addressing each issue.

3. Discuss the roles and responsibilities of collaborative team members in addressing each issue.

Resistance, Reflection, and Rationale

As you may recall from chapter 1, part of the job of your guiding coalition or leadership team includes leading staff through predicable turmoil. No matter how clear the communication or how compelling the evidence, some staff members will always resist living up to agreed-on collective commitments. The resistance often comes in the form of compromises. Following are some typical comments made by teachers attempting to avoid PLC work and expedite the learning process. Address each of the questions by providing the rationale for why each strategy is worth the time it takes to implement.

1. Can't I opt out of the collaborative team meetings as long as I am getting good results?

2. There are so many things I could be doing back in my classroom. I don't understand—why do we have to meet so much?

3. I'm not comfortable confronting other teammates about their behavior or not pulling their weight.

4. I don't feel the need to confront teammates because, ultimately, I'm going to get my work done anyway.

5. Couldn't we simply use the questions from the textbook to monitor student learning instead of working together to create common formative assessments?

6. I've been teaching this content long enough to know what my students need to be successful. I don't understand why we all have to agree on targets.

7. Do we really need to examine student achievement data if I know who is going to pass and fail before I give the assessment?

1 2 3 Not True of Our Team		4 5 Our Team Is Addressing This	6 7	8 9 10 True of Our Team
	Critical Issue	Rating	Role of the Principal	Role of Collaborative Teams
1	We have organized staff members into meaningful collaborative teams that support each member's daily responsibilities.			
2	We provide protected time for collaborative teams to meet on a weekly basis (if possible).			
3	We have identified team norms and protocols to guide us in working together.			
4	We have analyzed student achievement data and established SMART goals that we are working interdependently to achieve.			

Continued on next page ↓

Figure 6.1: Examining the critical issues in the Now.

	1 2 3 Not True of Our Team	4 5 6 7 Our Team Is Addressing This		8 9 10 True of Our Team
	Critical Issue	Rating	Role of the Principal	Role of Collaborative Teams
5	Each member of our team is clear on the essential learnings of our course in general as well as the essential learnings of each unit.			
6	We have aligned the essential learnings with state and district standards and the high-stakes exams required of our students.			
7	We have identified course content or topics that we can eliminate so we can devote more time to essential curriculum.			
8	We have agreed on how best to sequence the content of the course and have established pacing guides to help students achieve the intended essential learnings.			

	1 2 3 Not True of Our Team	4 5 6 7 Our Team Is Addressing This		8 9 10 True of Our Team
	Critical Issue	Rating	Role of the Principal	Role of Collaborative Teams
9	We have identified the prerequisite knowledge and skills students need in order to master the essential learnings of our courses and each of their units.			
10	We have identified strategies and created instruments to assess whether students have the prerequisite knowledge and skills.			
11	We have developed strategies and systems to assist students in acquiring prerequisite knowledge and skills when they are lacking in those areas.			
12	We have developed frequent common formative assessments that help us determine each student's mastery of essential learnings.			

Continued on next page ↓

	1 2 3 Not True of Our Team	4 5 Our Team Is Addressing This	6 7 Role of the Principal	8 9 10 True of Our Team Role of Collaborative Teams
	Critical Issue	Rating		
13	We have established the proficiency standard we want every student to achieve on each skill and concept that we examine with our common assessments.			
14	We have developed common summative assessments that help us assess the strengths and weaknesses of our program.			
15	We have established the proficiency standard we want every student to achieve on each skill and concept that we examine with our summative assessments.			
16	We have agreed on the criteria we will use to judge the quality of student work related to the essential learnings of our course, and we practice applying those criteria to ensure consistency.			

	1 2 3 Not True of Our Team	4 5 Our Team Is Addressing This	6 7	8 9 10 True of Our Team
	Critical Issue	Rating	Role of the Principal	Role of Collaborative Teams
17	We have taught students the criteria we will use to judge the quality of their work and have provided them with examples.			
18	We use the results of our common assessments to assist each other in building strengths and addressing weaknesses as part of a process of continuous improvement designed to help students achieve at higher levels.			
19	We use the results of our common assessments to identify students who need additional time and support to master essential learnings, and we work within the systems and processes of the school to ensure they receive that support.			
20	We evaluate our adherence to and the effectiveness of our team norms at least twice each year.			

Source: Courtesy of Tim Brown.

Visit **go.solution-tree.com/plcbooks** for a reproducible version of this figure.

8. Shouldn't students who fail to demonstrate proficiency suffer the consequences of failure rather than being provided with additional opportunities to learn?

9. Aren't systematic interventions enabling students?

10. Why do we need to give common formative assessments? We already know which students will pass and who will fail.

11. I'm afraid that my data are going to be used to judge or evaluate me. It's not fair. Not all students are the same.

Planning and Prioritizing Your Work

Based on the data and discussion from the critical issues activity, use the template in figure 6.2 to analyze and organize your data and plan your next steps. Consider the following questions when planning and prioritizing your work.

• What is our plan for follow-up after the initial introduction of the material, presentation, or training?

• What resources will we share to help stakeholders gain understanding?

• What problems or barriers can we anticipate?

• How will we obtain feedback from stakeholders?

Let's take a look at how one school used this resource to engage in the process of prioritizing next steps and identifying expectations for reciprocal accountability.

A School on the Rise: William B. Tecler Arts in Education Magnet School

Ken has done some high-impact work with the staff of William B. Tecler Arts in Education Magnet School in Greater Amsterdam, New York. Tecler was identified as a struggling school in need of improvement. Upon being appointed principal, Bethany Schill knew that PLC transformation was the greatest hope to empower teachers in a way that would allow for effective collaboration and improved

Area of Focus:			
Current Status	Preferred Status	What Steps Do We Need to Take and in What Order?	Who Will Do This and by When?
		Action one:	Action one:
		Action two:	Action two:
		Action three:	Action three:
		Action four:	Action four:
		Action five:	Action five:
		Action six:	Action six:

Figure 6.2: Template for planning and prioritizing work.

Visit go.solution-tree.com/plcbooks for a reproducible version of this figure.

teaching and learning. Ken had the honor and privilege of working with Tecler on a monthly basis for an entire school year support-ing the school's transformation. Tecler is now a school on the rise because the staff have elected to do what so many schools fail to do, and that is breathe life into their school's mission, and then live every day by that mission of learning for all. When asked of the impact at Tecler, Beth shared:

> This work helped to focus our building culture on student learning. We used this moral imperative to align actions of staff to represent this belief. Focused collaboration has helped staff to see value in taking ownership of all kids and not just those in the four walls of their classroom. (Bethany Schill, personal communication, May 5, 2015)

As you've learned throughout this book, identifying and commit-ting to your school's core purpose can be as challenging a process as it is a unifying process. At Tecler, there were additional obstacles to overcome as well. The public perception and reputation of the school were not ideal. Not only did some in the local community question why parents sent their kids there, but teachers were often questioned about why they would want to work at Tecler. While unearthing some of that history with staff, Ken discovered that there was a time years ago when Tecler was held in much higher regard in the community. What became clear quickly is that the collective esteem of the staff suffered along with student performance results. Ken used the process of authentic alignment with the staff to address both those challenges. Staff members needed to build more confi-dence based on their shared commitments and desired results, which were in their reach. There is a symbiotic relationship between the efficacy of educators and improvement in student learning.

The staff analyzed, planned, and prioritized the work they needed to do to get the results they desired, and they outlined what reciprocal accountability needed to look like at Tecler for the staff to meet its goals (see figure 6.3). Every school has unique needs and requirements. The examples in figure 6.3 illustrate how Tecler built reciprocal accountability around staff members' collective commitments and goals so that everyone could successfully deliver on expectations.

Behavioral Expectation/ Commitment of Collaborative Team	Principal Accountability
We will work within meaningful collaborative teams that support each member's daily responsibilities.	Provide opportunities for staff to build shared knowledge around how teacher collaboration is aligned with a learning-for-all culture. At Tecler, Beth provided opportunities to study and explore the research using articles and case studies. She also provided staff the opportunity to do their own research on the impact of teacher collaboration on student learning.
Collaborative teams are expected to meet on a weekly basis (if possible).	Beth convened with teacher leaders to revise the master schedule so that it would provide protected time for teams to meet on a weekly basis. The team developed some creative solutions that helped provide common planning time for teams.

Continued on next page →

Figure 6.3: Sample reciprocal accountability template.

Behavioral Expectation/ Commitment of Collaborative Team	Principal Accountability
Collaborative teams establish targets by analyzing student achievement data and getting clear on the most essential learnings of the course as well as the essential learnings of each unit. Teams align the essential learnings with state and district standards and the high-stakes exams required of students.	Beth used the work of Douglas Reeves and Robert Marzano to build team capacity to evaluate and prioritize standards. She also provided teams with a protocol for coming to consensus on the most essential targets (adapted from the work of Bailey & Jakicic, 2012).
Teams establish a short-term SMART goal of ensuring that 100 percent of students master the identified essential learning targets every quarter. They commit to work interdependently to achieve this goal and track and monitor progress toward this goal on a weekly basis.	Beth over-communicates her commitment to support the team working interdependently. Her feedback is always in the context of the team and the interdependent team goal. She provides the teams with visual tools (whiteboards, colored dots, magnets, space) to visually track student learning in real time.
Teams agree on how to best sequence the content of the course and establish pacing guides to help students achieve the intended essential learnings.	Beth provides teams with tools, such as an Essential Standards Chart and Calendar (adapted from Buffum et al., 2012), to effectively plan their courses and content.

It's not unusual for school leaders to look at some of what they're accountable for and feel confident that they can deliver on the resources, supports, and capacity building. With the role of school leader changing from management to instructional leader/change agent, leaders should also be prepared to encounter challenges that require their own capacity building. A common leadership myth is the expectation that the school principal has all the answers. Nothing can be further from the truth. As schools journey deeper into their transformation into PLCs, there will inevitably be opportunities for administrators to build capacity along with their staff. This is a great opportunity to live the mantra, "We all learn together." Being a model for continuous learning and transparency is a powerful way to communicate commitment to the shared mission of learning for all.

As of the printing of this book, the work at William B. Tecler continues. When asked about the impact of PLC transformation on her leadership, Beth shared:

> This process has completely transformed my leadership style. More than ever, I see the value in building teacher capacity, and there is a great opportunity for that to happen with the work of collaborative teams. We focus on collaboration with staff commitments. We have become strategic about implementing initiatives that support our PLC. There's no way I can improve learning for our students alone. My goal is to foster staff ownership. (Bethany Schill, personal communication, May 9, 2015)

Every change process is going to face challenges. While we have highlighted some aspects of cultural change at Tecler, we don't want to paint an unrealistic picture. There have been challenges, resistance, opportunities to redirect behavior, opportunities to challenge thinking, occasions to change direction, and distractions. Again, these challenges are to be expected. We asked Beth how she stays focused amidst challenges:

> Being committed with a laser-like focus on all students learning. Keeping our mantra at the forefront with staff so decisions move us toward our vision. Emphasizing opportunities for staff to share with each other, horizon-

tally and vertically. Recognizing small accomplishments to celebrate. (Bethany Schill, personal communication, May 9, 2015)

To that end, when you keep the Why of the work at the forefront of the Eye, Now, and How of the work, your path will stay lit.

Ensuring Learning for All

In an era when schools need to ensure all students learn at high levels amid competing priorities, increased demands, decreased resources, and desires of multiple stakeholders, it's more important now than ever that schools connect the deep, shared meaning they've developed as PLCs—the mission, vision, values, and goals—to the work they do. Because the world of teaching and learning is so dynamic, there are countless distractions. When the Why is not part of your daily work, identifying and maintaining your priorities is a challenge. You become susceptible to settling for the next best thing. The Now stage of authentic alignment encourages reflection and another layer of clarity in your work of building a culture of collective responsibility so you and your staff can focus on strengthening your PLC and ensuring high levels of learning for all students.

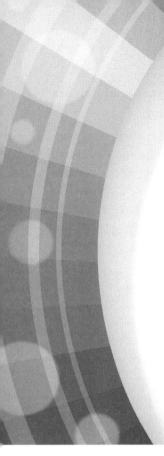

Chapter 7

Communication: Stories and Celebrations

The key to building our PLC wasn't presentations, but a thousand conversations— one at a time.

—PRINCIPAL IN A PLC

In the hustle and bustle that is the reality of schools today, leaders sometimes gloss over the importance of communication. They assume that the work is so crystal clear that everyone understands and is on board. To expect that learning will occur by osmosis is counterproductive to moving your PLC forward, and it also belies the fact that even the most ardent supporters need reminders. William Sommers (2006) states, "Sometimes leaders forget to restate, recommit, and rethink what we believe and value" (p. 7). This story helps illustrate the point.

Tom was asked to work with an elementary school on its overall culture and its academic and behavioral supports for students. He received background information on the staff. The staff had a nice blend of teaching experience, and everything seemed in order. When he arrived, he saw that the school walls were adorned with motivational quotes, there was a well-defined behavior matrix, the acronym GREAT described the school with each of the letters standing for something valued, and yet something was amiss. Their data indicated numerous office referrals, high rates of disciplinary action, and low academic results. Tom's first meeting with the staff revealed this disconnect. Taking a chance, he asked the group what the *E* in GREAT stood for. (He picked the one letter and word he thought would be easiest: *excellence*.) The question drew a lot of blank stares until one teacher, who had been in the school for over twenty years, ventured a guess. "I was here when we created that acronym, and I think it's *excellent*." No one else joined to support or refute her claim.

What is the moral of the story? In the absence of knowing, it's really hard to get to the doing. As Sommers (2006) advises, "Over-communicate organizational clarity" (p. 7). In this case, neither the leader nor the team communicated the need to connect the mission and vision or the current practice to the desired outcomes, and the *E* for excellence was just the beginning of their problems. One thing was said, another was done, and, potentially, a third was described on the posters. That disconnect led to varying views of expectations for students, and the overt efforts to ignore being GREAT.

We know from the workshops we have facilitated that educators love to talk, and we mean that in the most deeply respectful way. Whenever we provide talk time, we struggle to get participants to disengage from the meaningful conversations they are having with colleagues—in many instances colleagues they are meeting for the first time. This reminds us that educators want to be in the conversation about things that matter most. They are also willing to listen to the concerns of others. Margaret Wheatley (2002) reminds us that "large and successful change efforts start with conversations among friends, not with those in power" (p. 31).

In education, you need more information, connections, understanding, and collaboration. You can only accomplish this by opening, widening, and regularly traveling the channels of communication.

We can't think of anything that has given us more hope than to observe how simple, caring conversations give birth to powerful actions that improve chances for all students.

For conversation to take us to a deeper level of meaning and add value, Wheatley (2002) suggests the need to consider these principles:

> We acknowledge one another as equals, we try to stay curious about each other, we recognize that we need each other's help to become better listeners, we slow down so we have time to think and reflect, we remember that conversation is the natural way humans think together, we expect it to be messy at times. (p. 29)

Many of these principles run counter to how schools currently operate. Busy people with busy schedules populate schools. We rarely, if ever, encounter an educator with too much time and not enough activity in his or her school day. We question, however, when teams waste valuable time discussing tardiness, the hat policy, food or drink in class, and what day is best to have the next assembly. This time is better used for deep and meaningful dialogue that explores differences and similarities as staff members co-construct their future path.

As educators work together to chart this path, Wheatley (2002) suggests they need to include an ally that they may not have previously considered—"our willingness to be disturbed" (p. 34). She describes it as the capacity to endure challenges to our beliefs and engage in thinking that might produce a different outcome than one previously championed. She states that we should "acknowledge that everyone is an expert about something. Know that creative solutions come from new connections" (Wheatley, 2002, p. 145). In doing this, schools may achieve clarity for their next steps.

Effective communication travels two ways. Potent leaders are aware they have two ears and one mouth and use them proportionally. As

Kouzes and Posner (1987) remind us, "Communication pathways are the veins and arteries of new ideas" (p. 56). Ensuring that the flow in both remains unblocked is a vital strategy for leaders to employ. So how do schools strategically use the power of communication to focus primarily on the culture of collective responsibility? Storytelling and aligned celebration are two ways PLCs can intentionally strengthen communication.

Storytelling Shapes Culture

Whether you realize it or not, you already use storytelling as a tool in your school. People share stories about your school and the people within it privately and publicly in many settings: inside the school, outside the school, in the staff lounge, via text, on social media, in the local supermarket, at sporting events—pretty much everywhere. The great oral tradition of telling stories has been part of the human experience since the beginning of language. Our goal is to help you harness what already exists and direct its energy in a way that proves useful in your quest for a culture of collective responsibility. Harnessing the power of storytelling to reshape school culture is a vastly underutilized practice in schools. I once heard a colleague, Richard Dewey, remark, "He who tells the story, shapes the culture" (personal communication, 2009). Dewey's statement "hit us where we live," in the words of Ken's grandfather, Felix Cooks. It caused us to open our eyes and notice two things.

1. Every school has a story—for better or worse, positive or negative, true or untrue. People are telling stories about your site.

2. Every school has an opportunity to share the story it wants told.

One of our most powerful discoveries, one that we used in our schools, was this: if we wanted the story of our school to change, then we had to take responsibility to change it. We had to not only make commitments to do the essential work of a PLC as we've described in the process of connecting the How, but we had to be proactive in telling the stories: the breakthroughs, challenges, and setbacks, all aligned with the shared mission and vision. We were convinced that the story of our school would only change if *we* changed the story. But before we could do this, we had to be willing to take stock of the stories that shaped our current culture.

According to Kouzes and Posner (1999),

> Stories put a human face on success. They tell us that someone just like us can make it happen. They create organizational role models that everyone can relate to. They put the behavior in a real context and make standards more than statistics. Stories make standards come alive. (p. 105)

In the context of school culture, we would take this statement by Kouzes and Posner even further. Stories put a human face on actions we take that move us toward the culture we desire, as well as actions that move us away from it. Reshaping your culture to one of collective responsibility requires the powerful practice of storytelling to constantly and cyclically reinforce your values, commitments, beliefs, assumptions, and habits. These align with your school's mission that you further examined in the Why stage.

Early in the process of establishing storytelling in the culture of our schools, we sometimes got the ball rolling by sharing our own stories of overcoming challenges. We created opportunities for others to share in an attempt to integrate this practice. When you embed systems for storytelling, you guarantee many opportunities to share stories. While this facilitates storytelling at first, your goal is to incorporate the practice into the culture so all staff members contribute the kind of stories that reinforce the most important aspects of the shared mission and vision.

Inviting Engagement and Problem Solving

In their book *Made to Stick*, authors Chip and Dan Heath (2007) write about the power of stories to problem solve. They share the perspective of Steve Denning, leadership expert, author, and consultant. Denning is a huge advocate of the power of storytelling.

Denning defines a *springboard story* as a story that lets people see how an existing problem might change. Springboard stories tell people about possibilities. One major advantage of springboard stories is that they combat skepticism and create buy-in. He says that the idea of telling stories initially violated his intuition. He had always believed in the value of being direct, and he worried that stories were too ambiguous, too peripheral, and too anecdotal. He thought:

> Why not spell out the message directly? Why go to the trouble and difficulty of trying to elicit the listener's thinking indirectly, when it would be so much simpler if I come straight out in an abstract directive? Why not hit the listeners between the eyes? (Heath & Heath, 2007, Kindle location 3988)

The problem is, when you "hit listeners between the eyes" they often respond by fighting back. The way you deliver a message to them is a cue to how they should react. If you make an argument, you're implicitly asking them to evaluate your argument—judge it, debate it, criticize it—and then argue back, at least in their minds. But with a story, Denning argues, you engage the audience—you are involving people with the idea, asking them to participate with you. In addition to creating buy-in, springboard stories mobilize people to act. Stories focus people on potential solutions. Telling stories with visible goals and barriers shifts the audience into a problem-solving mode. Clearly, the amount of problem solving we do varies across stories (Heath & Heath, 2007).

We have a challenge for you: take a minute and recall the last meeting you attended where sharing data was the focus. We've all been to them—the PowerPoint slides seem to run together after a while because they're so riddled with numbers. Or you're so nervous about what the data will reveal that you can't concentrate on anything but that one slide. Now that you have recalled that meeting, take a moment and write down all you remember from the meeting about the data. Please be specific.

We're looking for specific details about the data. Are you scrambling to get something written? Did you skip the activity entirely?

Having trouble? Probably so. Now, think about the last meeting where a story was shared that moved you, one that impacted you then and now. Write down your reflections.

We guess that you have less information to share regarding the finer points of recent data and more information on a story that moved you. Every time we challenge a school with these two prompts, we are reminded that in our own professional lives, our meetings have been long on facts and data, and woefully short on stories that move us. How did we get to this place where we fall so short in what some argue is the oldest and most powerful form of sharing, the oral tradition?

Garr Reynolds (2008b) shares his thoughts on stories in a post on his blog *Presentation Zen* introducing Robert McKee's (1997) book *Story*:

> As children we were naturally good at telling stories about events or topics that mattered and learning from others via their stories, but as we became older we were taught that serious people relied only on presenting information and "the facts." Accurate information, sound logic, and the facts are necessary, of course, but truly effective leaders in any field—including technical ones—know how to tell "the story" of their particular research endeavor, technological quest, or marketing plan, etc.

Educators are no exception. Effective school leaders and teachers know how to tell the story of their school—its history, victories, challenges, crises, tragedies, and triumphs. Principals often struggle to connect with staff about school goals in a way that appeals to both the head and the heart. We refer to these as "slow down to speed up" strategies. You aim to deepen commitment and change behaviors, but it's easy to miss the important steps that feed and strengthen your school culture. This is something many change processes tend to neglect, but using stories to convey what is valued and important is an essential catalyst for truly changing behavior.

Moving From Polite to Provocative

An amazing phenomenon occurs when we guide schools through the authentic alignment process—a tipping point when the work moves from polite to provocative. It's usually around the time when we're helping a team examine its beliefs and assumptions, and then assisting them with seeing whether or not their behaviors, practices, and policies align with what they claim is most important. Our workshops are facilitative in nature, and as a result, we require a lot of participation. Attendees are predictably hesitant to share and be transparent. Through skillful facilitation, we eventually break through the awkward silence and make it safe for teams to be transparent. They begin sharing challenges, struggles, frustration, and concerns. And without fail, there is an almost collective sigh of relief around the room. You see teammates nodding in agreement.

When one team shares its story, others immediately relate. Some others offer support because they're experiencing the same challenges. Others recommend solutions because they've been through the same issues and have come out the other side. This happens during impromptu moments of sharing. You can imagine the power when you make storytelling part of your culture of collective responsibility. Kevin Eikenberry (2010) has identified five reasons why stories are such a powerful communication tool. As you read them, think about the countless number of opportunities to share stories aligned to your shared mission and vision. How you can use stories more effectively to deepen commitment to a culture of collective responsibility?

1. **Stories make a point.** Select your stories carefully and match them to your intended message. Don't tell stories just "because they are powerful," but rather because they help you make an important point.

2. **Stories make the point memorable.** Using well-selected, well-timed, and oft-repeated stories will help people remember your message.

3. **Stories make the point meaningful.** Use stories to create meaning for people; however, remember that not everyone will find exactly the same meaning. That's okay as long as you are telling your stories purposefully and making your main message clear. The meaning each person creates helps him or her remember and personalize the story.

4. **Stories create and reveal emotions.** Stories tap into part of what makes us all human. Remember that tapping into people's emotions will help to influence or persuade them.

5. **Stories build connections.** All stories can create a bond between the teller and the receiver; however, the strongest connections will be forged by personal, first-person stories. As a leader, remember your most powerful stories will be things you share about your life experience—especially a time when you failed or made a mistake.

While engaging in aligned storytelling, you must ensure the stories move your school toward a culture of collective responsibility. Aligned stories can do much to reinforce your shared mission, vision, and commitments to the essential work of a PLC. They communicate, teach lessons, and reflect the soul of your school. Stories from both individual and collective experience emphasize what is important and valued. They speak to us at the most basic level and connect with individuals in a way that data or slideshow presentations alone can't. For example, your staff may share:

- The story of how teachers at a once-failing school opened their minds to the idea of improvement from within, which supports the "Power of Collective Responsibility" guiding school mantra

- The story of how a very effective but resistant veteran teacher committed to the behaviors of a collaborative team hoping for results and benefits that would move him to believe in the idea, which reinforced the moral imperative of the How stage

- The story of a group of teachers who rallied to support a new teacher struggling with classroom management, which supports the "All Kids Are *Our* Kids" guiding school mantra

- The story of the school custodian who made time to visit with and mentor students, which supports the "All Hands on Deck" guiding school mantra
- The story of how a school arranged for a language interpreter for parent and PTA meetings, which supports the commitment to collective responsibility
- The story of a collaborative team of teachers who decided to be proactive and intentional about a student new to their grade level who had his first wildly successful year in school. The student arrived with a well-earned reputation for poor behavior and poor achievement. They shared a story of their noble intentions and some of the setbacks they experienced. This supports their vision of a school with "high ceilings, soft floors, and new opportunities for every student."

It's important to create an environment where people feel safe to share stories of both struggle and triumph. When you welcome stories that sometimes highlight the challenges and struggles of PLC transformation, you accomplish two important things:

- Not everything goes right all the time, even with the best of intentions. Setbacks and challenges are inherent parts of the PLC journey. You must continue to face and move in the direction of your mission. Remember that in toxic environments, stories that express frustration and setbacks might reinforce the negative aspects of the culture you're trying to leave behind. When you and your staff understand that there is no smooth road to any ideal worth pursuing, that is a sign your culture is healthy.
- When you share stories both aligned to and characterized by setbacks, you may prompt listeners to offer suggestions, support, or resources that might lead to a breakthrough. This practice also inherently reinforces collective responsibility.

It is important to embrace the fact that not all stories your leaders and teammates share will be success stories, and this is for a good reason. Sharing both the ups and downs of a school journey shows that you are all human, vulnerable, fallible, and thus relatable. For example, if budget cuts dictate that you soon must reduce staff, then they might share their experiences of how they handled a similar situation. This has the potential to turn what typically would be a complaint and excuse session to one of coping and problem solving. When you share your own concerns and stories, they become more relatable and human to those who work for and with them.

When you consider the entire PLC process, you'll discover unlimited opportunities to share stories along the journey. This is not to say that presenting quantitative data is unimportant; we simply mean that it should not be the sole method of communicating. Your stories must be relevant to the direction the school culture is moving for aligned storytelling to be a culture-building tool.

The following activity will help you understand the stories of your school and how they reflect the perceptions of it.

1. What stories do people tell about your school? What are the accompanying perceptions? Describe the stories that staff members, students, and parents share about your school. Once you've collected several examples, examine them for theme and suitability to continue as part of the fabric of your school culture.

   Consider the following questions individually and collectively as a team.

   • What is the most common perception of our school shared among staff?

   • What is the most common perception of our school shared among students?

   • What is the most common perception of our school shared among parents?

   • What is the most common perception of our school shared among district leadership?

2. Now assess these perceptions and determine which are aligned and misaligned with a culture of collective responsibility. Evaluate their meaning and impact. Now consider the following questions:

- Which of the collected stories help support and shape our desired school culture? What policies and practices do we observe that support these perceptions?

- Which stories have a negative message, are not aligned with our desired school culture, and should be replaced with new stories? What policies and practices do we observe that support these perceptions? What do we need to start doing to change these perceptions? What do we need to stop doing to change these perceptions?

As a leader, you must be vigilant about linking behaviors to shared mission, vision, and commitments if stories are to change them. Connecting the dots helps identify important behaviors and those you want to see repeated in an effort to shape or reshape your school's culture.

Aligned Celebration

If there is one area that tends to get short shrift in schools today, it is the time you devote to effective celebration and recognition. We often ask the educators we work with, "How many of you hear the words 'thank you' so much that you're sick of them?" The emphatic response always indicates that people never hear those words enough. In general, when it comes to genuine recognition and celebration, most people feel underappreciated and undervalued. Praise is rare in most workplaces. One poll found that an astounding 65 percent of Americans reported receiving no recognition for good work in the past year (Lombardo, 2014). Aligned celebration is powerful because you communicate recognition through your shared mission, vision, and commitment to the essential work of a PLC. It's an opportunity for everyone in the organization to observe and then recognize other teammates for actions that reinforce a culture of collective responsibility. You must allot time to acknowledging the achievements of individuals, teams, and the entire community in order to keep fueled the commitment to the essential work of a PLC.

The question of when to celebrate seems to perplex educators and often leads to its absence. The timing of the celebration isn't as critical as its rationale. Rather than wait for teammates to achieve some arbitrary threshold, focus on acknowledging those practices that move your school toward the desired results. Build in early celebrations to recognize early wins. If this work represents a departure from current practice and has your school embarking on a new journey, celebrate each toehold that you gain. In every moment of celebration, articulate the alignment to your school's guiding mantra. This provides clarity in terms of both expectations and accomplishments.

Another time-related issue that influences celebration is the notion that there isn't enough time for it. If you think celebration takes too much time, consider how much time lack of clarity or neglect of core values takes. How much time is lost to misalignment? How much time is lost when morale hits rock bottom and you must rally the troops for the next push?

Aligning celebration as a precursor ensures that the staff focus on the values they've identified as foundational to the work of their school. Work we did with a school district in Woodridge, Illinois, highlighted this practice. Greg Wolcott, assistant superintendent for teaching and learning in School District 68, wanted to highlight the first aspect of the district's FOCUS acronym (personal communication, July 19, 2013).

- Form strong, caring relationships with and between students.
- Operate with high expectations and clear targets in place.
- Create engagement through meaningful experiences.
- Utilize data to inform instructional planning.
- Supply specific and timely feedback to ensure each student achieves his or her personal best.

As a means of reminding everyone of the importance of relation-ships, the school year began with the *significant 72*. This referred to the first three days of school (or seventy-two hours) where everyone in the district would engage in activities that built relationships—student to student, student to adult, adult to student, and adult to adult. Here are two of the many activities that took place during those first three days.

During this activity that celebrated the unique attributes of students, teachers asked students to write words that describe them-selves on LEGO blocks. They discussed their descriptors with a peer and repeated that step for each block. The activity concluded with students building something as a group to illustrate that while they all possessed individual talents, together they could create some-thing special.

For the other activity, teachers made small stones with words on them (*friend, hope, leader*, and so on), put them in water, and then froze them to encase each stone in ice. The students broke the ice (a real icebreaker activity!) around each stone and talked about the attribute. Greg received numerous messages from each of the dis-trict schools about how these activities celebrating students' positive attributes were a hit. Follow-up celebrations throughout the year also aligned with this key idea of celebrating positive attributes. If you intend to form strong, caring relationships, what would it look like and how would it translate to daily, weekly, and yearlong prac-tice? When teachers get to know their students, they can personalize their teaching and place students in an environment where they want to learn. Greg followed the significant 72 model at the start of the school year along with shorter versions (seventy-two minutes or seventy-two seconds) on a monthly, weekly, and daily basis.

In order to emphasize the connections made during the initial three days, teachers made envelopes and strips of paper available throughout the school. Whenever anyone in the school community witnessed anyone else in the school community doing something that emphasized or built a connection, he or she wrote that person's name on the strip of paper and presented it to him or her. When the recipient went to his or her next class, the teacher asked if anyone had good news to share. Students read the strips, a standing ovation followed, and the strip was taken to the office where it became another link in the friendship chain. When the chain extended around the main hallway of the school, the principal bought all students a treat.

These celebrations increased the likelihood that emphasizing relationships would become simply the way things are done. This district didn't just stumble onto the notion that a focus on celebrating relationships would significantly impact student learning. Staff members' anecdotal analysis two months into the school year revealed that discipline referrals and tardiness decreased while academic outcomes improved. These findings are consistent with a meta-analysis (Durlak, Weissberg, Dymnicki, Taylor, & Schellinger, 2011) that involved over two hundred schools and more than 270,000 students in kindergarten through high school. These students "demonstrated significantly improved social and emotional skills, attitudes, behavior, and academic performance that reflected an 11-percentile-point gain in achievement" (Durlak et al., 2011 p. 405). The starting point was to identify a key attribute. Emphasizing it through celebration supports positive growth, and aligning it to demonstrated actions embeds it in the culture of a school and district.

Matawan-Aberdeen Middle School principal Cory Radisch shared with us how his staff work to embed aligned celebration in their culture. One thing they do is start each meeting with something called check-ins, meaning five minutes of celebrations. Just like the contractor who says, "No job too big or too small," check-ins emphasize small victories just as much as the big ones. This allows meetings to begin with a positive vibe and validates the hard work teachers do on a daily basis. Imagine starting your meetings with several rounds of applause as you celebrate a student increasing his or her reading level or another student's winning essay. Check-ins are a simple way to remind you and your staff why you do what you do.

Another celebration method Cory uses is what they call perk cards. The school mascot is a husky, so administrators deliver Husky Hero cards to teachers at meetings or in mailboxes. These cards are a way for them to recognize teachers for meeting and exceeding expectations by acting as a *merchant of hope* for their students. Once a teacher receives a card, he or she can turn it in for various incentives. Some of the incentives include:

- A morning beverage of choice delivered by an administrator
- Breakfast
- A day off from a duty
- A pass to come in late or leave early
- A front parking space (especially in the winter months)

Cory also uses Twitter to celebrate and recognize staff and students. Celebratory tweets range from acknowledgments of sporting events and concerts to appreciation of the great instruction and learning going on in classrooms. The latter piece is critical. Teachers on Twitter can see the tweets, but he also follows up with an email thanking them for their hard work.

The use of celebrations is extremely important to help change and shape the culture. In Cory's current school, turnover in administration led to a culture of mistrust and apprehension. However, by celebrating the accomplishments of teachers and students, administrators helped form a culture that is slowly changing from "us versus them" to a culture where it's "all for one and one for all," regardless of title. Celebrations allow teachers to feel honored at a time when public perceptions may paint a different picture. Most importantly, celebrating and honoring the miracle moments and accomplishments of teachers and students helps educators realize that their purpose far outweighs their challenges. The biggest difference it made for Cory's school is the growth of an unwavering appreciation for the Why, which makes the How much more manageable in an ever-changing profession (Cory Radisch, personal communication, May 2014).

Aligned celebration helps sustain the momentum for change, validates the initiators and movers, and convinces the holdouts that the work is worth the struggle. It draws staff together to acknowledge their own efforts and to enjoy time together in a less structured environment. Cynthia Zarate (2006) suggests,

> Remembering to recognize, reward, and celebrate accomplishments is a critical leadership skill. And it is probably the most underutilized motivational tool in organizations. There is no limit to how much recognition you can provide, and it is often free. Recognition brings the change cycle to its logical conclusion, but it also motivates people to attempt change again. (p. 166)

Effective leaders who take the time to pause in the moment can nurture some of the most vital needs of human beings—competency, being valued, relationships, and feeling significant. Ignoring these needs and forgetting to celebrate while on this journey may result in the loss of momentum and a reversion to compliance—to just doing as one is told. We have taken various routes with our own teams over the years to recognize their hard work. We've consistently seen a deeper connection to each other, to the work at hand, and ultimately to the success of our students.

Your staff can use the template in figure 7.1 (page 160) to align their celebrations with the school mission and vision. Without this focus, you may spend time celebrating things that don't move you toward your desired culture. (It's okay to hold celebrations that don't relate to mission and vision, but for authentic alignment, celebration should be focused.) You can customize the form with your school's logo, colors, and so on.

Aligned Celebration Form

I would like to recognize _____ for _____ .

His or her actions reflect a culture of collective responsibility because:

_____

_____

_____

_____

Given by: _____   Date: _____

Figure 7.1: Sample aligned celebration form.

*Visit **go.solution-tree.com/plcbooks** for a reproducible version of this figure.*

Taking Stock

Taking stock of perceptions, aligning storytelling, and aligning celebration are high-leverage strategies to intentionally shape your school's culture. Examining perceptions from various stakeholder groups is important for assessing your school's current reality. Storytelling is one of the oldest forms of communication in human history, and one of the most underutilized strategies used today. Celebrations are important links to the shared mission and vision and a way to focus on behaviors aligned with collective responsibility. Make celebrations everyone's responsibility and get people involved in planning them. Joint planning offers social support, encourages people to laugh together, and generates more creativity than asking one person to handle everything.

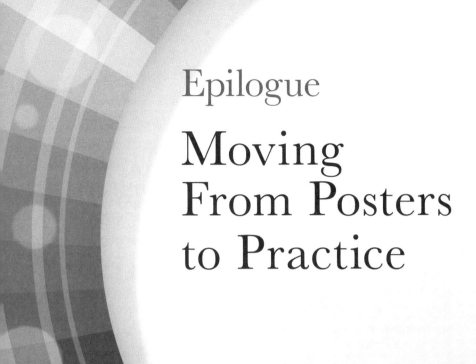

Epilogue

Moving From Posters to Practice

Marketing experts claim you should be able to explain what you do in under thirty seconds. When asked the purpose of this book, our under-thirty-second response is "We help schools live their posters; we help them move from posters to practice."

We developed the authentic alignment model to strengthen and support the four foundational pillars of a PLC. Having implemented the PLC model in our own schools, and facilitated the process in many others, we saw a very common problem: the deep meaning behind the work (mission and vision) and the deep implementation of the work (values and goals) were often mutually exclusive, and nothing can be further from the truth. While schools addressed the four pillars, they were rarely deeply embedded as a part of the school culture. Without this connection, schools are not set up to ensure high levels of learning for all students within a culture of collective responsibility.

The fact is, school systems typically look to new programs, initiatives, and strategies without examining their fundamental beliefs, core values, and the school's fundamental purpose. Schools must get beyond implementation primarily out of compliance, and move toward implementing initiatives because they see the need for a culture of collective responsibility. A close and proactive examination with the Why, Eye, How, and Now helps in that endeavor.

If you put in the time and energy to use the authentic alignment process, it will support the work of your PLC. The commitment to ensuring high levels of learning for all students is challenging work. Students benefit when their schools are purposeful places that not only clearly define what they want all students to know and be able to do but also clearly describe how they are going to bring about these desired results and how they will know if they have succeeded.

When schools are in sync about their fundamental purpose, clear about the picture of what they want to become as a school, firm about their collective commitments, and also prioritize their next steps, there is a collective confidence that bubbles to the surface. Not only are people more confident about the prospect of breakthrough achievement, they are more confident about taking aligned action to achieve their goals. We can take risks and try things in a safe environment because we're all on the same page about what we believe and where our school is going. Being in sync with everyone around you provides powerful psychological benefits. It fosters what you want in a PLC: action orientation and experimentation.

When we look around and are surrounded by like people who believe what we believe, and we've taken steps to publicly identify and declare those beliefs in an effort to move in the same direction, it also gives us the confidence to try new things and pursue new goals. The role of a leader is not to come up with all the great ideas; the role of a leader is to create an environment in which great ideas can happen. Authentic alignment is a tool to help create and sustain your PLC environment where great achievement can happen.

Travelers in centuries past looked to the stars to find the right path. And so it is with the business of teaching and learning. It's about keeping what you believe and what you decide is most important front and center. When we have the honor of working with groups for professional development, one of the most highly rated aspects of our work is the opportunity to talk together. Participants acknowledge time after time that they don't get enough opportunities to dialogue about their work. This phenomenon is less about the lack of time, and more about a lack of focus and attention. If you deem dialogue to be important, then you make time for it. Margaret Wheatley (2002) supports this assertion when she contends:

> We can also take courage from the fact that many people are longing to be in conversation again. We are hungry for a chance to talk. People want to tell their story, and are willing to listen to yours. People want to talk about their concerns and struggles. Too many of us feel isolated, strange, or invisible. Conversation helps end that. (p. 24)

Where can we find the courage to start a good conversation? The answer is found in the word itself. *Courage* comes from the old French word for heart (*cuer*). We develop courage for those things that speak to our heart (Wheatley, 2002). The things that speak to the heart of the school are found in the Why. Everything that matters with regard to moving schools forward in the direction of high levels of learning emanates from the Why. The Why represents those things that we hold with conviction. And our courage grows for things that affect us deeply, things that open our hearts. Once our heart is engaged, it is easy to be brave. We only need enough courage to invite teammates to a conversation—a conversation that begins from the inside out. A conversation that starts with our Why beliefs, the compelling vision of our ideal school we examine in the Eye, the collective commitments of the How, and in the focused action of the Now.

William Damon (2008) suggests that purpose provides the route to excellence: "Only when students discover personal meaning in their work do they apply their efforts with focus and imagination" (p. 10). We are willing to take the risk of extending Damon's suggestion to the work of educators and schools as well. We assert that the route to learning excellence, the learning excellence of both students and adults, is formed when educators discover personal meaning in their work and apply their efforts with focus and imagination, coming to consensus about their school's shared purpose and commitments.

Simon Sinek (2009) asserts that there are many ways to motivate people to do things, but deep commitment comes from the ability to inspire people. All we want is for our colleagues to have their incredible efforts rewarded by results. It is our hope that this book facilitates the process of digging beneath the surface, developing your school's lens, which, when aligned with all other work, will allow all learners to flourish. Remember your shared mission, your shared vision, your shared commitments, and your shared purpose. These gifts, strengths, skills, attributes, and passion are always there. They make your school the one your students have been waiting for.

References and Resources

Abrahams, J. (1995). *The mission statement book: 301 corporate mission statements from America's top companies.* Berkeley, CA: Ten Speed Press.

ACT. (2013). *2012 retention/completion summary tables.* Accessed at http://act.org/research/policymakers/pdf/12retain_trends.pdf on August 19, 2013.

Ainsworth, L. (2013). *Prioritizing the Common Core: Identifying specific standards to emphasize the most.* Englewood, CO: Lead + Learn Press.

Allen, L. (2001). From plaques to practice: How schools can breathe life into their guiding beliefs. *Phi Delta Kappan, 83*(4), 289–293.

Bailey, K., & Jakicic, C. (2012). *Common formative assessment: A toolkit for Professional Learning Communities at Work.* Bloomington, IN: Solution Tree Press.

Barber, M., & Mourshed, M. (2009, November). *Shaping the future: How good education systems can become great in the decade ahead— Report on the International Education Roundtable.* Singapore: McKinsey & Company. Accessed at www.academia.edu/3627965 /Education_Roundtable on March 19, 2015.

Barth, R. S. (2006). Improving relationships within the schoolhouse. *Educational Leadership, 63*(6), 8–13.

Bass, B. M. (1985). *Leadership and performance beyond expectations.* New York: Free Press.

Bennis, W. (1997). The secrets of great groups. *Leader to Leader, 1997*(3), 29–33.

Blanchard, K. (2007). *Leading at a higher level: Blanchard on leadership and creating high performing organizations.* Upper Saddle River, NJ: Pearson/Prentice Hall.

Boyer, E. L. (1995). *The basic school: A community for learning.* San Francisco: Jossey-Bass.

Brounstein, M. (2000). *Coaching and mentoring for dummies.* Foster City, CA: IDG Books.

Bryk, A. S., Sebring, P. B., Allensworth, E., Luppescu, S., & Easton, J. Q. (2010). *Organizing schools for improvement: Lessons from Chicago.* Chicago: University of Chicago Press.

Buffum, A., Mattos, M., & Weber, C. (2012). *Simplifying response to intervention: Four essential guiding principles.* Bloomington, IN: Solution Tree Press.

Bureau of Labor Statistics. (2013). *Education and training outlook for occupations, 2012–2022.* Washington, DC: U.S. Department of Labor. Accessed at www.bls.gov/emp/ep_edtrain_outlook.pdf on November 13, 2014.

Burns, J. M. (1978). *Leadership.* New York: Harper & Row.

Canfield, J. (2005). *The success principles: How to get from where you are to where you want to be.* New York: HarperCollins.

Carroll, T. G., Fulton, K., & Doerr, H. (Eds.). (2010, June). *Team up for 21st century teaching and learning: What research and practice reveal about professional learning.* Washington, DC: National Commission on Teaching and America's Future.

Collins, J. (2005). *Good to great and the social sectors: Why business thinking is not the answer.* New York: HarperCollins.

Connors, R., & Smith, T. (2011). *Change the culture, change the game: The breakthrough strategy for energizing your organization and creating accountability for results.* New York: Portfolio.

Conzemius, A. E., & Morganti-Fisher, T. (2012). *More than a SMART goal: Staying focused on student learning.* Bloomington, IN: Solution Tree Press.

Covey, S. R. (with Merril, R. R.). (2006). *The speed of trust: The one thing that changes everything.* New York: Free Press.

Covey, S. R., Merrill, A. R., & Merrill, R. R. (1994). *First things first: To live, to love, to learn, to leave a legacy.* New York: Simon & Schuster.

Damon, W. (2008). The moral North Star. *Educational Leadership, 66*(2), 8–13.

Darling-Hammond, L. (1996). What matters most: A competent teacher for every child. *Phi Delta Kappan, 78*(3), 193–200.

Deal, T. E., & Key, M. K. (1998). *Corporate celebration: Play, purpose, and profit at work.* San Francisco: Berrett-Koehler.

DuFour, R. (2004). Leading edge: Are you looking out the window or in a mirror? *Journal of Staff Development, 25*(3), 63–64.

DuFour, R., DuFour, R., & Eaker, R. (2008). *Revisiting Professional Learning Communities at Work: New insights for improving schools.* Bloomington, IN: Solution Tree Press.

DuFour, R., DuFour, R., Eaker, R., & Karhanek, G. (2004). *Whatever it takes: How professional learning communities respond when kids don't learn.* Bloomington, IN: Solution Tree Press.

DuFour, R., DuFour, R., Eaker, R., & Karhanek, G. (2010). *Raising the bar and closing the gap: Whatever it takes.* Bloomington, IN: Solution Tree Press.

DuFour, R., DuFour, R., Eaker, R., & Many, T. (2010a). *Learning by doing: A handbook for Professional Learning Communities at Work* (2nd ed.). Bloomington, IN: Solution Tree Press.

DuFour, R., DuFour, R., Eaker, R., & Many, T. (2010b). *Learning by doing: A handbook for Professional Learning Communities at Work* (2nd ed.)—*Action guide.* Accessed at http://pages.solution-tree. com/rs/solutiontree/images/LBD_StudyGuide.pdf%20 on June 18, 2015.

DuFour, R., & Eaker, R. (1998). *Professional Learning Communities at Work: Best practices for enhancing student achievement.* Bloomington, IN: Solution Tree Press.

DuFour, R., & Marzano, R. J. (2011). *Leaders of learning: How district, school, and classroom leaders improve student achievement.* Bloomington, IN: Solution Tree Press.

Durlak, J. A., Weissberg, R. P., Dymnicki, A. B., Taylor, R. D., & Schellinger, K. B. (2011). The impact of enhancing students' social and emotional learning: A meta-analysis of school-based universal interventions. *Child Development, 82*(1), 405–432.

Eaker, R., & Keating, J. (2008). A shift in school culture: Collective commitments focus on change that benefits student learning. *Journal of Staff Development, 29*(3), 14–17.

Eikenberry, K. (2010, October 11). *Five reasons stories are a powerful communication tool* [Blog post]. Accessed at http://blog.kevineikenberry.com/leadership/five-reasons-stories-are-a-powerful-communication-tool on March 9, 2014.

Eisaguirre, L. (2007). *The power of a good fight: Embracing conflict to drive productivity, creativity, and innovation* (Exec. ed.). Indianapolis, IN: Literary Architects.

Eli and Edythe Broad Foundation. (n.d.). *Statistics.* Accessed at http://broadeducation.org/about/crisis_stats.html on August 20, 2013.

Eliason, T. (2008, December 1). Coveted wisdom: Stephen Covey, a highly effective leader. *Success.* Accessed at www.success.com/article/coveted-wisdom on February 18, 2015.

Elmore, R. F. (2004). *School reform from the inside out: Policy, practice, and performance.* Cambridge, MA: Harvard Education Press.

Elmore, R. F. (2010). "I used to think . . . and now I think . . .": Reflections on the work of school reform. *Harvard Education Letter, 26*(1), 8.

Epstein, J. L., & Sheldon, S. B. (2002). Present and accounted for: Improving student attendance through family and community involvement. *Journal of Educational Research, 95*(5), 308–318.

Fryer, B. (2003). Storytelling that moves people: A conversation with screenwriting coach Robert McKee. *Harvard Business Review, 81*(6), 51–55.

Fullan, M. (2005). *Leadership and sustainability: System thinkers in action.* Thousand Oaks, CA: Corwin Press.

Fullan, M., & St. Germain, C. (2006). *Learning places: A field guide for improving the context of schooling.* Thousand Oaks, CA: Corwin Press.

Gabriel, J. G., & Farmer, P. C. (2009). *How to help your school thrive without breaking the bank.* Alexandria, VA: Association for Supervision and Curriculum Development.

Gallimore, R., Ermeling, B. A., Saunders, W. M., & Goldenberg, C. (2009). Moving the learning of teaching closer to practice: Teacher education implications of school-based inquiry teams. *Elementary School Journal, 109*(5), 537–553.

Garmston, R. J., & Wellman, B. M. (1999). *The adaptive school: A sourcebook for developing collaborative groups.* Norwood, MA: Christopher-Gordon.

Glickman, C. D. (1993). *Renewing America's schools: A guide for school-based action.* San Francisco: Jossey-Bass.

Goleman, D. (2002). Leading resonant teams. *Leader to Leader, 2002 (25)*, 24–30.

Gordon, T., & Edwards, W. S. (1995). *Making the patient your partner: Communication skills for doctors and other caregivers.* Santa Barbara: Greenwood Publishing Group.

Great Schools Partnership. (2014). *The glossary of education reform.* Accessed at http://edglossary.org/mission-and-vision on July 15, 2014.

Guskey, T. R. (2011). Five obstacles to grading reform. *Educational Leadership, 69*(3), 16–21.

Hamel, G. (2000). *Leading the revolution: How to thrive in turbulent times by making innovation a way of life.* Cambridge, MA: Harvard Business School Press.

Handy, C. (1995). Managing the dream. In S. Chawla & J. Renesch (Eds.), *Learning organizations: Developing cultures for tomorrow's workplace* (pp. 45–56). New York: Productivity Press.

Hansen, M. V., & Allen, R. G. (2002). *The one minute millionaire: The enlightened way to wealth.* New York: Harmony Books.

Hattie, J. (2012). Know thy impact. *Educational Leadership, 70*(1), 18–23.

Hernandez, D. J. (2012). *Double jeopardy: How third-grade reading skills and poverty influence high school graduation.* Baltimore: Annie E. Casey Foundation. Accessed at www.aecf.org/m/resourcedoc /AECF-DoubleJeopardy-2012-Full.pdf on July 15, 2014.

Heath, C., & Heath, D. (2007). *Made to stick: Why some ideas survive and others die* [Kindle version]. New York: Random House.

Heath, D. (2010, March 10). *How to write a mission statement that doesn't suck* [Video file]. Accessed at www.fastcompany.com/1404951 /How-write-mission-statement-doesnt-suck-video on September 12, 2013.

Hierck, T. (2009). Differentiated pathways to success. In T. R. Guskey (Ed.), *The teacher as assessment leader* (pp. 249–262). Bloomington, IN: Solution Tree Press.

Hierck, T., Coleman, C., & Weber, C. (2011). *Pyramid of behavior interventions: Seven keys to a positive learning environment.* Bloomington, IN: Solution Tree Press.

Hilliard, A. (1977). Classical failure and success in the assessment of people of color. In M. W. Coleman (Ed.), *Black children just keep on growing: Alternative curriculum models for young black children.* Washington, DC: National Black Child Development Institute.

Hirsh, S. (1996). *Seeing and creating the future.* Oxford, OH: National Staff Development Council.

Hirsh, S. (2012). A professional learning community's power lies in its intentions. *Journal of Staff Development, 33*(3), 64.

Hsu, J. (2008). The secrets of storytelling: Why we love a good yarn. *Scientific American Mind, 19*(4), 46–51.

Hulley, W., & Dier, L. (2005). *Harbors of hope: The Planning for School and Student Success Process.* Bloomington, IN: Solution Tree Press.

Jackson, Y. (2011). *The pedagogy of confidence: Inspiring high intellectual performance in urban schools* [Kindle version]. New York: Teachers College Press.

Jerald, C. D. (2009, July). *Defining a 21st century education.* Alexandria, VA: Center for Public Education.

Joyce, B., & Showers, B. (1995, May). Learning experiences in staff development. *The Developer, 3.*

Kanold, T. D. (2011). *The five disciplines of PLC leaders.* Bloomington, IN: Solution Tree Press.

Kanter, R. M. (2005). How leaders gain (and lose) confidence. *Leader to Leader, 2005*(35), 21–27.

Katzenbach, J. R., & Smith, D. K. (1993). *The wisdom of teams: Creating the high-performance organization.* Boston: Harvard Business School Press.

Kawasaki, G. (2004). *The art of the start: The time-tested, battle-hardened guide for anyone starting anything.* New York: Portfolio.

Kirtman, L. (2013). *Leadership and teams: The missing piece of the educational reform puzzle.* Boston: Pearson.

Kotter, J. P. (2010). *Eight steps for leading change.* Accessed at www.kotterinternational.com/kotterprinciples/ChangeSteps/Step2.aspx on March 15, 2011.

Kotter, J. P., & Cohen, D. S. (2002). *The heart of change: Real-life stories of how people change their organizations.* Boston: Harvard Business School Press.

Kouzes, J. M., & Posner, B. Z. (1987). *The leadership challenge: How to get extraordinary things done in organizations.* San Francisco: Jossey-Bass.

Kouzes, J. M., & Posner, B. Z. (1999). *Encouraging the heart: A leader's guide to rewarding and recognizing others.* San Francisco: Jossey-Bass.

Kouzes, J. M., & Posner, B. Z. (2006). *A leader's legacy.* San Francisco: Jossey-Bass.

Kouzes, J. M., & Posner, B. Z. (2009). To lead, create a shared vision. *Harvard Business Review, 87*(1), 20–21.

Kruse, K. (2012, October 16). 100 best quotes on leadership. *Forbes.* Accessed at www.forbes.com/sites/kevinkruse/2012/10/16 /quotes-on-leadership on March 9, 2014.

Kruse, S. D., Louis, K. S., & Bryk, A. S. (1995). An emerging framework for analyzing school-based professional community. In K. S. Louis, S. D. Kruse, et al. (Eds.), *Professionalism and community: Perspectives on reforming urban schools* (pp. 23–42). Thousand Oaks, CA: Corwin Press.

Lacour, M., & Tissington, L. D. (2011). The effects of poverty on academic achievement. *Educational Research and Reviews, 6*(7), 522–527.

Lassiter, C. J. (2012). *The secrets and simple truths of high-performing school cultures.* Englewood, CO: Lead + Learn Press.

Lencioni, P. M. (2003). The trouble with teamwork. *Leader to Leader, 2003*(29), 35–40.

Levin, H. M., & Rouse, C. E. (2012, January 25). The true cost of high school dropouts. *New York Times.* Accessed at www.nytimes .com/2012/01/26/opinion/the-true-cost-of-high-school-dropouts .html?_r=1&nl=todaysheadlines&emc=thab1 on September 12, 2013.

Lezotte, L. W., & McKee, K. M. (2002). *Assembly required: A continuous school improvement system.* Okemos, MI: Effective Schools Products.

Little, J. W. (2006, December). *Professional community and professional development in the learning-centered school.* Washington, DC: National Education Association. Accessed at www.nea.org/assets /docs/HE/mf_pdreport.pdf on September 12, 2013.

Lombardo, E. (2014). *Better than perfect: 7 strategies to crush your inner critic and create a life you love.* Berkeley, CA: Seal Press.

Louis, K. S., Kruse, S. D., & Marks, H. M. (1996). Schoolwide professional community. In F. M. Newmann et al. (Eds.), *Authentic achievement: Restructuring schools for intellectual quality* (pp. 179–203). San Francisco: Jossey-Bass.

Louis, K. S., Leithwood, K., Wahlstrom, K. L., & Anderson, S. E. (2010, July). *Investigating the links to improved student learning: Final report of research findings.* New York: Wallace Foundation.

MacNeil, A. J., Prater, D. L., & Busch, S. (2009). The effects of school culture and climate on student achievement. *International Journal of Leadership in Education, 12*(1), 73–84.

Many, T. W. (2009). What's on your refrigerator door?: Clarifying what really matters in your school. *TEPSA News,* 8–9.

Marzano, R. J. (2003). *What works in schools: Translating research into action.* Alexandria, VA: Association for Supervision and Curriculum Development.

Marzano, R. J., Kendall, J. S., & Gaddy, B. B. (1999). *Essential knowledge: The debate over what American students should know.* Aurora, CO: McREL.

McClanahan, E., & Wicks, C. (1993). *Future force: Kids that want to, can, and do!—A teacher's handbook for using TQM in the classroom.* Chino Hills, CA: Pact.

McCormack, F. (2006). Mind games. *Scholastic Scope, 54*(10), 14–16.

McDonald, J. P., Mohr, N., Dichter, A., & McDonald, E. C. (2007). *The power of protocols: An educator's guide to better practice* (2nd ed.). New York: Teachers College Press.

McKee, R. (1997). *Story: Substance, structure, style, and the principles of screenwriting.* New York: HarperCollins.

MetLife. (2012, March). *The MetLife survey of the American teacher: Teachers, parents and the economy.* New York: Author. Accessed at http://files.eric.ed.gov/fulltext/ED530021.pdf on June 18, 2015.

Mills, E. (2012, August 23). *Taglines, slogans and mantras? Itsy bitsy stories* [Blog post]. Accessed at www.claxonmarketing.com/2012/08/23/taglines-slogans-and-mantras-itsy-bitsy-stories on July 15, 2014.

Morrissey, M. S. (2000). *Professional learning communities: An ongoing exploration.* Austin, TX: Southwest Educational Development Laboratory. Accessed at www.sedl.org/pubs/change45/plc-ongoing.pdf on February 18, 2015.

Muhammad, A. (2009). *Transforming school culture: How to overcome staff division*. Bloomington, IN: Solution Tree Press.

Muir, M. (2012, August 8). *Building a shared vision part 1: Where to begin?* [Blog post]. Accessed at http://multiplepathways.wordpress.com/2012/08/08/building-a-shared-vision-part-1-where-to-begin on September 12, 2013.

National Board for Professional Teaching Standards. (n.d.). *Five core propositions*. Accessed at www.nbpts.org/five-core-propositions on February 18, 2015.

National Center for Education Statistics. (2009). *The Nation's Report Card: Reading 2009* (NCES 2010-458). Washington, DC: Institute of Education Sciences.

National Council of Teachers of English. (2006, April). *NCTE principles of adolescent literacy reform: A policy research brief*. Urbana, IL: Author. Accessed at www.ncte.org/library/NCTEFiles/Resources/PolicyResearch/AdolLitPrinciples.pdf on February 18, 2015.

National Council of Teachers of Mathematics. (2008). *Principles and standards for school mathematics*. Reston, VA: Author.

National Science Teachers Association. (2006). *NSTA position statement: Professional development in science education*. Accessed at www.nsta.org/about/positions/profdev.aspx on February 18, 2015.

Neason, M. (2012, August 8). The power of visualization. *Sport Psychology Today*. Accessed at www.sportpsychologytoday.com/sport-psychology-for-coaches/the-power-of-visualization on February 18, 2015.

Noguera, P. (2003). *City schools and the American dream: Reclaiming the promise of public education*. New York: Teachers College Press.

O'Guinn, C. M., Giani, M. S., & Geiser, K. (2010). *Renewing school: Productive dialogue and difficult conversations*. Accessed at www.stanford.edu/dept/SUSE/gardnercenter/docs/YiM_WA4_Productive_Talk_Difficult_Conversations.doc on July 15, 2014.

Ordóñez, L. D., Schweitzer, M. E., Galinsky, A. D., & Bazerman, M. H. (2009). *Goals gone wild: The systematic side effects of over-prescribing goal setting* (Working Paper No. 09-083). Boston: Harvard Business School Press.

Organisation for Economic Co-operation and Development. (2009). *Education at a glance 2009: OECD indicators.* Paris: Author.

Organisation for Economic Co-operation and Development. (2013). *Education at a glance 2013: OECD indicators.* Paris: Author.

Patterson, K., Grenny, J., Maxfield, D., McMillan, R., & Switzler, A. (2008). *Influencer: The power to change anything.* New York: McGraw-Hill.

Peters, T., & Austin, N. (1985). *A passion for excellence: The leadership difference.* New York: Random House.

Pfeffer, J., & Sutton, R. I. (2000). *The knowing-doing gap: How smart companies turn knowledge into action.* Boston: Harvard Business School Press.

Power, B. (2014, April 26). *The big fresh: Are we still serving hamburgers?* Accessed at www.choiceliteracy.com/articles-detail-view.php?id=1995 on July 15, 2014.

Rath, T., & Clifton, D. O. (2004). *How full is your bucket?: Positive strategies for work and life.* New York: Gallup Press.

Reeves, D. B. (2002). *The leader's guide to standards: A blueprint for educational equity and excellence.* San Francisco: Jossey-Bass.

Reeves, D. B. (2004). *Accountability in action: A blueprint for learning organizations* (2nd ed.). Englewood, CO: Advanced Learning Press.

Reeves, D. B. (2005). Putting it all together: Standards, assessment, and accountability in successful professional learning communities. In R. DuFour, R. Eaker, & R. DuFour (Eds.), *On common ground: The power of professional learning communities* (pp. 45–63). Bloomington, IN: Solution Tree Press.

Reeves, D. B. (2006). *The learning leader: How to focus school improvement for better results.* Alexandria, VA: Association for Supervision and Curriculum Development.

Reeves, D. B. (2008). Leading to change / Improving student attendance. *Educational Leadership, 65*(8), 90–91.

Reeves, D. B. (2010). *Transforming professional development into student results*. Alexandria, VA: Association for Supervision and Curriculum Development.

Reina, D. S., & Reina, M. L. (2006). *Trust and betrayal in the workplace: Building effective relationships in your organization* (2nd rev. ed.) [Kindle version]. San Francisco: Berrett-Koehler.

Reynolds, D., & Teddlie, C. (2000). The processes of school effectiveness. In C. Teddlie & D. Reynolds (Eds.), *The international handbook of school effectiveness research* (pp. 134–159). New York: Routledge.

Reynolds, G. (2008a). *Presentation Zen: Simple ideas on presentation design and delivery*. Berkeley, CA: New Riders.

Reynolds, G. (2008b, July 19). *Robert McKee on the power of story* [Blog post]. Accessed at www.presentationzen.com/presentationzen/2008/07/robert-mckee-on-the-power-of-story.html on July 15, 2014.

Robbins, P., & Alvy, H. B. (2004). *The new principal's fieldbook: Strategies for success*. Alexandria, VA: Association for Supervision and Curriculum Development.

Robbins, P., & Alvy, H. B. (2009). *The principal's companion: Strategies for making the job easier* (3rd ed.). Thousand Oaks, CA: Corwin Press.

Roberts, S. M., & Pruitt, E. Z. (2009). *Schools as professional learning communities: Collaborative activities and strategies for professional development* (2nd ed.). Thousand Oaks, CA: Corwin Press.

Scaglione, R., & Cummins, W. (1990). *Karate of Okinawa: Building warrior spirit*. New York: Person-to-Person.

Schaffer, R. H. (2010). Four mistakes leaders keep making. *Harvard Business Review, 88*(9), 86–91, 126.

Scherer, M. (2001). How and why standards can improve student achievement: A conversation with Robert J. Marzano. *Educational Leadership, 59*(1), 14–18.

Schlechty, P. C. (1997). *Inventing better schools: An action plan for educational reform*. San Francisco: Jossey-Bass.

Schmoker, M. J. (1996). *Results: The key to continuous school improvement.* Alexandria, VA: Association for Supervision and Curriculum Development.

Senge, P., Kleiner, A., Roberts, C., Ross, R., & Smith, B. (1994). *The fifth discipline fieldbook: Strategies and tools for building a learning organization.* New York: Currency.

Sherman, S., & Kerr, S. (1995, November 13). Stretch goals: The dark side of asking for miracles. *Fortune.* Accessed at http://archive.fortune.com/magazines/fortune/fortune_archive/1995/11/13/207680/index.htm on July 15, 2014.

Sinek, S. (2009). *Start with why: How great leaders inspire everyone to take action.* New York: Portfolio.

Sleigh, M. J., & Ritzer, D. R. (2001). Encouraging student attendance. *APS Observer, 14*(9), 19–20, 32–33.

Snow, S. (2012, August 9). *Repeat after me: Your company needs a mantra* [Blog post]. Accessed at www.fastcompany.com/3000236/repeat-after-me-your-company-needs-mantra on July 15, 2014.

Sommers, W. (2006). Now's the time to make a fresh start. *Journal of Staff Development, 27*(4), 7.

Stephenson, S. (2009). *Leading with trust: How to build strong school teams.* Bloomington, IN: Solution Tree Press.

Stoll, L. (1998). School culture. *School Improvement Network's Bulletin, 9.*

Stoll, L., Bolam, R., McMahon, A., Thomas, S., Wallace, M., Greenwood, A., et al. (2006). *Professional learning communities: Source materials for school leaders and other leaders of professional learning.* Nottingham, England: National College for School Leadership. Accessed at http://dera.ioe.ac.uk/16497/1/professional-learning-communities-01-user-guide.pdf on March 19, 2015.

Tavernise, S. (2012, September 20). Life spans shrink for least-educated whites in the U.S. *New York Times.* Accessed at www.nytimes.com/2012/09/21/us/life-expectancy-for-less-educated-whites-in-us-is-shrinking.html?pagewanted=all&_r=0 on September 12, 2013.

Timperley, H. (2008). *Teacher professional learning and development* (Educational Practices Series No. 18). Brussels, Belgium:

International Academy of Education. Accessed at www.ibe.unesco .org/fileadmin/user_upload/Publications/Educational_Practices /EdPractices_18.pdf on February 18, 2015.

Ulrich, D. (1996). Credibility x capability. In F. Hesselbein, M. Goldsmith, & R. Beckhard (Eds.), *The leader of the future: New visions, strategies, and practices for the next era* (pp. 209–220). San Francisco: Jossey-Bass.

Urwin, R. C., & Connolly, C. (2006). *The D-myth: Exposing the causes of depression and unleashing a new you.* Boise, ID: Mind Matters International.

Van Clay, M., Soldwedel, P., & Many, T. W. (2011). *Aligning school districts as PLCs.* Bloomington, IN: Solution Tree Press.

Vision. (n.d.). In *Merriam-Webster's online dictionary.* Accessed at www .merriam-webster.com/dictionary/vision on March 12, 2015.

Wahlstrom, K. L., & Louis, K. S. (2008). How teachers experience principal leadership: The roles of professional community, trust, efficacy, and shared responsibility. *Educational Administration Quarterly, 44*(4), 458–495.

Washington, J. M. (Ed.). (1986). *A testament of hope: The essential writings and speeches of Martin Luther King, Jr.* San Francisco: Harper & Row.

Whalan, F. (2012). *Collective responsibility: Redefining what falls between the cracks for school reform.* Boston: Sense.

Wheatley, M. J. (2002). *Turning to one another: Simple conversations to restore hope to the future.* San Francisco: Berrett-Koehler.

Wiliam, D. (2012). Feedback: Part of a system. *Educational Leadership, 70*(1), 30–34.

Williams, K. C. (2012). *Creating physical and emotional security in schools* (2nd ed.). Bloomington, IN: Solution Tree Press.

Zarate, C. A. (2006). *Organizational behavior and management in Philippine organizations.* Manila, Philippines: Rex Book Store.

Index

Cultures Built to Last
Richard DuFour, Michael Fullan
Take your professional learning community to the next level! Discover a systemwide approach for re-envisioning your PLC while sustaining growth and continuing momentum on your journey. You'll move beyond pockets of excellence while allowing every person to be an instrument of lasting cultural change.
BKF579

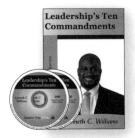

Leadership's Ten Commandments
Kenneth C. Williams
Looking for an easy-to-implement and powerful framework for leading and sustaining change in your professional learning community? Kenneth employs research, encourages audience participation, and reflects on his own experience to show you how to lead with integrity and create a collaborative staff dedicated to student learning.
DVF042

Making Teamwork Meaningful
William M. Ferriter, Parry Graham, and Matt Wight
Focus on developing people—not just improving test scores. The authors examine how staffing decisions can strengthen professional learning communities and explore actions that can help school leaders safeguard their schools against complacency.
BKF548

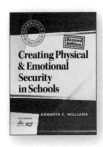

Creating Physical & Emotional Security in Schools
Kenneth C. Williams
Give your students a physically and emotionally safe learning environment. Learn how you and your teachers can nurture supportive relationships with students, develop conflict management strategies, prevent different forms of bullying, develop student initiative and resilience, and encourage celebration.
BKF451

Solution Tree | Press
a division of
Solution Tree

Visit solution-tree.com or call 800.733.6786 to order.